"The typical church serves i
for detailed but disconnect
book *The Connection of Chris*.,
missing link, a view of the "forest" that reveals the strong connections between biblical books, events, and characters. Such a perspective enables her readers to understand and to appreciate the many biblical details."

– Ivan Parke, Ph.D., Professor,
Department of Christian Studies and Philosophy,
Mississippi College,
co-author of *Reclaiming the Real Jesus*

"It is a mystery for many to see how the sixty-six books of the Bible are related to each other through Jesus Christ. Sandra Betz has given us a way to do this through her book *The Connection of Christ from Garden to Cross*. Use this book as a companion to your Bible study as you follow the story of Jesus Christ from Genesis to Revelation."

– Homer Walkup, Pastor,
Lake Shore Baptist Church,
Lake Dallas, Texas

"*The Connection of Christ from Garden to Cross* leads you directly to the heart of God. God loves you, and He wants you to know that He loves you."

– Betty Wolfe, Veteran Bible Teacher

"I have read many Bible study books in my life which address specific subjects. This book is unique in that it has given me an entirely new perspective on how to study the Bible as a whole and how each story in the Bible is interconnected. I now have a much broader view of the study of the Bible!!"

– Debra Martin, Bible Study Enthusiast

*You will seek me and find me
when you seek me with all your heart*
(Jeremiah 29:13).

The Connection of Christ
from Garden to Cross

SANDRA BETZ

WESTBOW
PRESS®
A DIVISION OF THOMAS NELSON
& ZONDERVAN

Copyright © 2015 Sandra Betz.

All rights reserved. No part of this book may be used or reproduced by any means, graphic, electronic, or mechanical, including photocopying, recording, taping or by any information storage retrieval system without the written permission of the publisher except in the case of brief quotations embodied in critical articles and reviews.

This book is a work of non-fiction. Unless otherwise noted, the author and the publisher make no explicit guarantees as to the accuracy of the information contained in this book and in some cases, names of people and places have been altered to protect their privacy.

Unless otherwise noted, all Scripture is taken from the New International Version.

Scripture taken from the HOLY BIBLE, NEW INTERNATIONAL VERSION®, Copyright © 1973, 1978, 1984 by International Bible Society. Used by permission of Zondervan Publishing House. All rights reserved.

The "NIV" and "New International Version" trademarks are registered in the United States Patent and Trademark Office by International Bible Society. Use of either trademark requires the permission of International Bible Society.

Where noted, Scripture is taken from the King James Version.

WestBow Press books may be ordered through booksellers or by contacting:

WestBow Press
A Division of Thomas Nelson & Zondervan
1663 Liberty Drive
Bloomington, IN 47403
www.westbowpress.com
1 (866) 928-1240

Because of the dynamic nature of the Internet, any web addresses or links contained in this book may have changed since publication and may no longer be valid. The views expressed in this work are solely those of the author and do not necessarily reflect the views of the publisher, and the publisher hereby disclaims any responsibility for them.

Any people depicted in stock imagery provided by Thinkstock are models, and such images are being used for illustrative purposes only. Certain stock imagery © Thinkstock.

ISBN: 978-1-4908-8641-1 (sc)
ISBN: 978-1-4908-8642-8 (hc)
ISBN: 978-1-4908-8640-4 (e)

Library of Congress Control Number: 2015910291

Print information available on the last page.

WestBow Press rev. date: 08/05/2015

Editorial Team

Joining me in editing this book has been an outstanding group of editors. Each one has brought a different talent to the pages.

Ivan Parke, Ph.D.
Professor, Department of Christian Studies and Philosophy, Mississippi College
Reclaiming the Real Jesus, co–author

Homer Walkup
Pastor, Lake Shore Baptist Church, Lake Dallas, Texas
More than 50 years in the ministry

Betty B. Wolfe
Veteran Bible Teacher
Over 40 years of teaching experience

Debra Martin
Bible Study Enthusiast

Amy Wolfe
Senior Technical Editor
SAS Institute Inc
Raleigh, North Carolina

Todd Betz
My wonderful husband

Acknowledgements

Thank you, Heavenly Father, for giving me the desire to dig. Please keep the tools in my hands and the desire in my heart.

Thank you, Debra Martin, for being my first reader. Another huge thank you to Dr. Ivan Parke, Pastor Homer Walkup, and Amy Wolfe for your professional guidance. Also thank you to Gene Anders for your expertise with the images. To the many friends at Lake Shore Baptist Church in Lake Dallas, Texas, thank you for your encouragement through the years of writing, rewriting, and editing. I could not have finished without you.

A very special thank you to my family for the time and patience you have given me through this journey: Love you Todd, Tejay, Matthew, and Dad and Mom (Don and Betty Wolfe).

"We did it, Mom! What an unforgettable journey."

Dedicated to my two sons, Tejay and Matthew, and the love of my life, my husband, Todd.

Contents

Preface xiii
Introduction xix

Chapter 1: Starting with the Basics 1
  What Is the Bible? 1
  How Was the Bible Written? 3
  Why Was the Bible Written? 3
  How Was the Bible Put Together? 5

Chapter 2: Building the Skeleton 11
  I. Creation to Abraham 14
  II. Abraham to Moses 16
  III. The Exodus and the Years of Wandering 18
  IV. The Conquest of Canaan 18
  V. The Judges 19
  VI. The Kingdom of Israel 19
  VII. The Divided Kingdom 21
  VIII. The Southern Kingdom of Judah Alone 22
  IX. The Captivity of Judah 22
  X. The Restoration of Israel 23

  Between the Testaments 24

  XI. Life of Christ 25
  XII. The Establishment of the Early Church 28

Chapter 3: Adding Meat to the Skeleton 31
  The Old Testament 32
  I. Creation to Abraham 32
    A. Creation 32

B. The Fall 35
  C. Cain and Abel... 37
  D. The Flood.. 37
  E. Confusion of Tongues 39
II. Abraham to Moses.. 40
  A. Abraham and His Wanderings................................... 40
  B. Isaac–the Son of Promise.. 45
  C. Jacob and His Twelve Sons 47
  D. Joseph–The Deliverer... 51
  E. Israel in Egypt... 54
III. The Exodus and the Years of Wandering 54
IV. The Conquest of Canaan 59
V. The Judges.. 64
VI. The Kingdom of Israel.. 66
  A. Saul's Reign... 67
  B. David's Reign.. 69
  C. Solomon's Reign 72
VII. The Divided Kingdom... 74
VIII. The Southern Kingdom of Judah Alone...................... 76
IX. The Captivity of Judah 77
X. The Restoration of Israel 78

Between the Testaments... 81

The New Testament.. 83
XI. Life of Christ 84
XII. The Establishment of the Early Church........................ 91
  A. The Period of Waiting for the Holy Spirit 92
  B. The Time of Pentecost 92
  C. The Persecution 93
  D. The Spread of the Gospel 97

Recognizing the Message 101
Now It Is Your Turn to Do the Digging............................. 103

Appendix **105**
    From Me to You 107
    Chart 1: Division of the Books of the Bible 109
    Chart 2: Books of the Bible by Historical Period 109
    Chart 3: Bible Chronological History Chart 110
    Short Overview of the Historical Books of the Bible 113
    Guide for Reading the History of the Bible 117

Preface

A Note to the Reader

What a pleasure it has been to pen this book. It is special to me because the work began with my precious mother. Ever since I can remember, Mom has been a Bible teacher. When I was young, she taught elementary-aged children during Sunday school. By the time I was in middle school, she was teaching high school girls. That was many years ago, but to this day, many of those now grown women remember her with fondness and speak of her love for the Lord. Shortly after she began teaching the older girls, she was asked to teach a women's Bible study. Often while I was away at school, groups of women met in our livingroom studying different books of the Bible that she had enjoyed studying.

Some time back in the early 1980s, Mom came to realize that she knew many bits and pieces of the Bible but felt she was missing something in the whole picture. It was plain that Christ was the thread that tied the books together, but she did not understand how all the stories fit together to show the story of Christ and His love for us. Curious to know more, Mom started what would become a ten-year journey to dig out the *big picture* of the Bible. When she was finished, she had compiled a thirteen page teaching outline that she called *The Bible Overview*. Of course, I have no doubt there were many pages of notes and knowledge from previous studies used, but all I ever saw was the thirteen pages. Those years of studying taught her how all those stories fit together to tell God's love for us and how they all point to God's desire to have a relationship with us, His creation. The insight gained from taking the time to sort out the Bible was apparent in her life. Her passion became sharing what she had learned. By this time, I was living far from home and unable to attend any of her studies. Phone conversations or brief visits were not sufficient to help me comprehend what she had learned. I struggled to grasp what she was saying.

Sometime in the mid-1990s, she gave me a copy of the thirteen pages and told me that someday she thought I might want to study them. I remember looking at those few words and saying right back to her, "How am I supposed to get an overview of the Bible in just thirteen pages?!" Literally, there was not one complete sentence! The information was notes in outline form! Because I was not able to understand what she had learned by talking to her, I seriously doubted that a brief outline would make comprehension any easier. She responded by telling me that I had to dig it out for myself. This was not something that she could tell me or fully write down. If I wanted to see the big picture of the Bible, I was going to have to dig it out for myself. The brief outline would serve as a guide to give me direction in where to dig. Deep down I wanted to know what she had uncovered, but at the time, I was not willing to put in the work. Honestly, I wanted the easy way out. I wanted her easy-to-read unabridged edition! So, without much thought, except for thinking my mom was a little nuts, I dropped her thirteen pages into a folder and filed it away—secretly hoping someday I would feel differently. But, I had my doubts. Off and on for the next ten years, I would run across those thirteen pages, and every time, I would shake my head. I would then file them back into the folder and forget about them until the next time. It was not until 2007 that God finally got ahold of me, and I pulled the outline out never to hide it in the dark recesses of the filing cabinet again. God knew I had to be prepared for such a dig.

Shortly after I filed my mom's outline the first time, I attended my first Beth Moore Bible study entitled *A Women's Heart: God's Dwelling Place*.[1] This study centered on the tabernacle that God had Moses build, where He could dwell among His people. But the knowledge of the tabernacle I gained extended well beyond the confines of the building itself. Its relevance stretched all the way to the cross in the New Testament. I saw the tabernacle as the picture to mankind of our need for a savior. From that moment of revelation, I was on fire! I further recognized the story of the Israelites, the descendants of Abraham, as a picture of God calling us back into relationship with Him. Before I knew it, the Old Testament was alive with relevance to New Testament living. Through most of that study, I was calling my mom nightly sharing with her how I was seeing the connection between the Old Testament and the New Testament. The Bible was coming together, and an excitement was growing inside me that was difficult to contain. I could see glimpses of the big picture and wanted to see more. It was then that I was asked to teach a women's Bible study. Teaching further increased my appetite, but it would take a few more years to gain confidence for a full-fledged dig into *The Bible Overview*.

By the spring of 2007, I had spent several years teaching and becoming a sponge for God's Word. But, I had never attempted to teach a study that I had prepared. Planning for the fall study, I was unsure of what to teach. I spent time browsing through Christian book stores reading various studies, but none seemed to be the right fit. In the back of my mind, I had been thinking about *The Bible Overview*. Beth Moore's study had remained heavy on my mind, and my curiosity to know more was intensifying. After several dead ends, I pulled out my mother's thirteen pages and without as much as a pause, I picked up my Bible and started to dig.

At the time, my oldest son was working at a dinosaur dig site. There was much excitement as they dug up bones because with each find, they were putting together a fossilized dinosaur! I felt that same thrill studying, but the bones I was digging up were coming together to reveal a different kind of skeleton—a skeleton of the Bible. But instead of fossilized, each find was part of a living, breathing message from God. To me, it was the living skeleton of the Bible. When I say skeleton, I mean the basic foundation of the Bible. I discovered that grouping the history books into historical periods laid a foundation for all the stories to fall into a chronological order. Once placed, the stories connected together to give God's message of the Bible from the Garden to the cross and beyond. As my excavation deepened, it became clearer what my mother was talking about when she said the big picture. The deeper I dug, the more defined the skeleton became. After six months, I had finally gone through the thirteen pages and expanded them into thirty-seven, plus a notebook full of additional information. I had uncovered the skeleton of the Bible that clearly revealed the thread—Jesus Christ. He was there at creation in the Old Testament, and His mercy reached all the way to the cross in the New Testament. Once I could picture the skeleton, no matter what study or sermon I listened to, I could see the basic foundation of the Bible in my mind, and I could tag the study or sermon to where it fit on the skeleton. Instead of each story being in and of itself, I saw how the stories connected together. This side of Heaven I will never be able to fill in the whole skeleton, but with each new truth I learn, a bit more meat is put on the skeleton.

By the time I completed the dig of my mother's overview, it was time to begin the fall study. I could think of nothing I wanted to teach more than *The Bible Overview*. God's Word had become alive in my soul, and I was excited to share my findings with as many as would listen. During the next year, I had the pleasure of teaching the study several times. I thoroughly enjoyed watching the women as they uncovered the skeleton for themselves and gained a better understanding of the Bible's message.

It was not long before I developed a deep desire to share this knowledge with my children. I could think of no better legacy to give them. I knew that it would be nearly impossible to sit down with them and walk them through the study. My oldest was thirteen, and my youngest was only nine at the time. Instead, I decided to write a book so they would have something to keep with them long after I am gone. In the beginning days of writing, I thought it would take only months to pen the words, but months turned into years. My mother told me that she never felt led to write the book because she knew it would be difficult. I did not realize how true that was until I found myself working on it almost eight years. The road to completion has not been easy. Early manuscripts were too wordy and hard to follow. But through time, God has been gracious in helping me find the words to convey my findings of the most exciting story I have ever read. Another blessing through this experience has been my mother joining me in editing the manuscript.

Somewhere along the way, I started dreaming about publishing. How exciting to think that my mother's curiosity has blossomed into helping so many understand the big picture of the Bible. I pray you enjoy this book. But more importantly, as you read, I hope you recognize how each story and each verse is God calling you to Him. The reason for the Bible is for us to learn that God loves us and His desire is to have a relationship with us.

---

[1] Moore, Beth. *A Women's Heart God's Dwelling Place.* Nashville, Tenn.: Lifeway Press, 1995.

Introduction

Let me understand the teaching of your precepts;
then I will mediate on your wonders
(Psalm 119:27).

Have you ever heard the story of Joseph and the coat of many colors? How about the story of Noah building a boat for his family and at least two of every creature to ride out a rainstorm that lasted for forty days? One of my favorites is the story of Elijah, who rode up to Heaven in a flaming chariot. Most people would recognize these stories from the pages of the Bible. Growing up and attending Sunday school, I heard these stories and many more. But as I grew into an adult, I wondered how all these stories connected together into God's plan for mankind. God chose men to write the Bible, but He was in control of what was written. The Bible states in 2 Timothy 3:16, "All Scripture is God breathed." So, why did God choose these particular stories to be canonized into the Bible? Thus, in my mid–40s, my dig to uncover the big picture began.

Since I came to know the Lord, I have understood that Christ came to earth to die on the cross for you and me, but what I did not understand was how all the stories of the Bible fit together to share this truth. To me, God's Word was very complex and confusing. Reading through from cover to cover could not hold my attention. Even though I knew it was God's Word and worthy of reading, I felt it was beyond my comprehension. This left me only with stories and verses that I had heard in Sunday school and truths learned listening to sermons. Sadly, I was missing the connections! Not until I was encouraged by my mother to dig into the Bible did I reach a point where I could begin to grasp the basic foundation of the Bible. It was so basic but rich with life that I came to see it as the living skeleton of the Bible. The more I dug, the more I discovered how the stories weave together to reveal why we need a savior and who is our Savior. Since this discovery, it has been my goal in life to share my findings of how the beautiful Bible stories share God's love and desire for a relationship with mankind. Maybe you have not been able to find God's message that flows from Genesis to Revelation. My hope is to show you the skeleton that will enable you to visualize for yourself the message of God's Word. The Bible truly is a love letter that not only is worthy of reading but can also be understood by you and me.

Chapter 1

Starting with the Basics

Show me your ways, O LORD, teach me your paths;
guide me in your truth and teach me,
for you are God my Savior,
and my hope is in you all day long
(Psalm 25:4–5).

To understand the message of the Bible, it is necessary to read it. However, for most people, reading the Bible through is challenging. Many of the books are not placed in chronological order, which tends to make for a difficult read. It is, therefore, advantageous to become familiar with God's Word before you can expect to gain understanding from it. When you have some familiarity of *what* the Bible is, *how* the Bible was written, *why* the Bible was written, and *how* the books fit together, the message becomes clearer.

What Is the Bible?

To answer this question, it might be easier to define what the Bible is not. First, the Bible is not a science book, even though several stories in the Bible discuss unusual scientific phenomena. For example, when Moses led the Israelites out of the land of Egypt, the Red Sea divided for the Israelites to cross and flee the Egyptians on dry land (Exod. 14:16, 21–22), but the Bible does not explain how the sea divided. That was not important to the message. What is important is *who* caused it to occur. Exodus 14:21–22 declares, "Then Moses stretched out his hand over the sea, and all that night the LORD drove the sea back with a strong east wind and turned it into dry land. The waters were divided, and the Israelites went through the sea on dry ground, with a wall of water on their right and on their left." Clearly, Scripture reveals God pulled back the waters. Another event that is even more spectacular is creation (Gen. 1–2). The Bible does not state a timeline or the specifics of how our planet came into being. Instead, the message of the Bible is concerned with *who* the creator is. In Genesis 1:3, it states, "And God said." The message is God spoke creation into existence. God is the *who*.

Second, the Bible is a history book but not just a history book. Through the pages of the Old Testament, we read about the history and development of God's chosen people. In the books of Genesis through Esther, the reader can follow the journey of God's people from their beginning to their return to Jerusalem during the captivity under the Mede-Persians. Although much of the history of the people is written, many historical facts are withheld. This is because the writings concerning the Israelites are not to reveal who the people were as a nation, but to reveal who God is to mankind.

Since the Bible is neither a science book nor just a history book, what is it? It is a book about God dealing with man. It is a story that reveals who God is and His relationship to man. From the beginning, God walked in fellowship with man in the garden. But when man chose to disobey God by eating the forbidden fruit, the relationship between God and man was broken—sin was birthed. Sin is disobedience to God. The Bible is God's love letter calling His children back into fellowship with Him through repentance, which is turning from sin and seeking God. It is each individual's decision to respond. How will you respond? Will you turn to Him or will you ignore your Creator's loving call back into fellowship?

How Was the Bible Written?

God spoke through men to record His message to mankind. I doubt very seriously the writers realized their manuscripts would be canonized into what later would be called the Bible, God's Holy Word. Instead, I surmise the writers were just being obedient to God's calling. These manuscripts were written over a period of fifteen hundred years. More than forty different writers penned the Bible, including kings, poets, prophets, musicians, philosophers, farmers, teachers, a priest, a statesman, a sheepherder, a tax collector, a physician, and a couple of fishermen. Even with all the different personalities writing the texts, God was the orchestrator who directed all the thoughts of the writers. 2 Peter 1:21 declares, "For prophesy never had its origin in the will of man, but men spoke from God as they were carried along by the Holy Spirit." Another reference to God's authorship is 2 Timothy 3:16–17, which states, "All Scripture is God-breathed and is useful for teaching, rebuking, correcting and training in righteousness, so that the man of God may be thoroughly equipped for every good work." God inspired and guided the writers. Their words became the message straight from His heart. Through time, these chosen historical scrolls, letters, and treatises became our Bible. God loved us so much that through these various writers, God wrote a letter to us in His own words.

Why Was the Bible Written?

The Bible was written to reveal four main truths. First, the Bible was written so that we might know who God is. He is the Creator (Gen. 1:1) and Sovereign Lord (1 Chron. 29:11–12). God created all things, and He knows all things.

Second, the Bible shows why we need a savior. "For all have sinned and fall short of the glory of God" (Rom. 3:23). In the book of James, the Bible says, "For whoever keeps the whole law and yet stumbles at just one point is guilty of breaking all of it" (James 2:10). Each individual faces punishment of spiritual death for his sin (Rom. 6:23). This means separation from God for all eternity. God chose the Israelites to show the world that man needs a savior to die for his sins. This makes it possible for man to have a relationship with the Most Holy God (John 14:6). God gave the Israelites the Law to live in obedience to Him (Deut. 4:1–2) and established the institution of sacrifice for the cleansing of sin (Heb. 9:22), but the Israelites on their own could not remain righteous (Gal. 2:15–16). They kept turning from God by being disobedient to His Law. The story of the Israelites is a picture of mankind showing that on our own, we are incapable of being free of sin. We need a savior, a perfect sacrifice, to make us righteous.

The third truth is what God has done for us. Man needed a permanent sacrifice, a savior. God gave us His Son as a perfect sacrifice for our sins (Heb. 7:27). "We have been made holy through the sacrifice of the body of Jesus Christ once for all" (Heb. 10:10). The acceptance of Jesus's death on the cross as a sacrifice for our sin enables us to have a permanent relationship with God. John 14:6 tells us, "Jesus answered, 'I am the way and the truth and the life. No one comes to the Father except through me.'"

Finally, the fourth truth found in the Bible is what God requires of believers. Acceptance of Christ's sacrifice comes with responsibility. We become His heirs—His children. Ephesians 4:11–13 states, "It was he who gave some to be apostles, some to be prophets, some to be evangelists and some to be pastors and teachers, to prepare God's people for works of service, so that the body of Christ may be built up until we all reach unity in the faith and in the knowledge of the Son of God and become mature, attaining to the whole measure of the fullness of Christ." Meaning, God has work on this earth for us to do. As Jesus told His disciples before He ascended into Heaven, we are to tell others about Jesus in our homes, communities, and across the world (Matt. 28:18–20). Being obedient on earth to God prepares us for the work He has for us in Heaven, where one day we will live with Him in eternity. Each of these truths is expounded on throughout the Bible.

How Was the Bible Put Together?

Now that we are familiar with *what* the Bible is, *how* it was written, and *why* it was written, we need to discover *how* the Bible was put together. The Bible consists of two parts: the Old Testament and the New Testament. The Old Testament was written in Hebrew and some Aramaic, and the New Testament was written in Greek. The word *testament* means "covenant," which is best defined as a promise from one person to another. The old covenant refers to the covenant made by God with Abraham, the father of Israel (Gen. 12:1–3). The New Testament shares the new promise that God made through Jesus Christ that is inclusive for all people. "For this reason Christ is the mediator of a new covenant, that those who are called may receive the promised eternal inheritance—now that he has died as a ransom to set them free from the sins committed under the first covenant" (Heb. 9:15). The Old Testament looks forward to the coming of the Savior, while the New Testament tells the story of His coming.

The books of the Bible are arranged into six different groups, which aids in comprehending the message God has for us. Use "Chart 1: Division of the Books of the Bible" (see page 108) in the appendix to help visualize these divisions. Notice there are sixty-six books of the Bible. Of these sixty-six books, thirty-nine are found in the Old Testament, and twenty-seven compose the New Testament. The thirty-nine books of the Old Testament are divided into three major groups: history, poetry, and prophecy. Similarly, the New Testament is divided into three major groups: history, letters, and prophecy. Even though a book is considered in a certain group, it does not mean that it is exclusive to that group. Many of the Minor Prophets are written in poetic prose. For example, Hosea is a book of poetry, but its message is prophecy. Therefore, it is considered largely a book of prophecy. The grouping is not exact; it is used as a method to help better grasp the purpose of each of the books.

Let us take a closer look at the two testaments, starting with the Old Testament. Keep in mind, the Old Testament was to show why we need a savior. Beginning with the first book of the Old Testament, Genesis, and reading through to the book of Esther takes you through the Old Testament books of history. With only a few exceptions, they are organized in chronological order, starting with man's beginning in the garden to the restoration of Israel. The first exception is Leviticus, which was written to explain what duties were expected of the priests and the people. The books of 1 and 2 Chronicles are also exceptions. These two books, written as one originally, are unique in that they cover the history from Saul's death to the time of the Judean captivity. They repeat much of the history found in 1 and 2 Samuel and 1 and 2 Kings, but tell the story from a priestly perspective to emphasize the line of David as the chosen people of God. Many scholars agree that 1 and 2 Chronicles were written during the time of the Judean captivity to remind the Jewish nation that God had taken care of them and was with them and would be with them in the years ahead. The final exception to the chronological order is the book of Esther, which is a story that fits into the time period of Ezra.

The next group of books found in the Old Testament is the five books of poetry, starting with Job and ending with Song of Solomon. These books express the full range of human emotions from human depression to jubilant trust in God. They are considered the books of humanities. Written during the period of the Old Testament, they bring to life the people of the time.

The seventeen books of prophecy from Isaiah to Malachi complete the Old Testament. They were written before and during captivity, prophesying the fate of the Southern Kingdom of Judah, the Northern Kingdom of Israel, and other countries if they did not turn back to God. They also contain prophecies about the coming of the Messiah. Isaiah prophesied, "For to us a child is born, to us a son is given, and the government will be on his shoulders. And he will be called Wonderful Counselor, Mighty God, Everlasting Father, Prince of Peace. Of the increase of his government and peace there will be no end. He will reign on David's throne and over his kingdom, establishing and upholding it with justice and righteousness from that time on and forever. The zeal of the LORD Almighty will accomplish this" (Isa. 9:6–7). Other books make reference to His coming, but Isaiah is the most prophetic.

Between the testaments is a period of some four hundred years, commonly known as the "silent years." This history is not spoken of in the Bible except through a few prophetic words found mostly in the books of Isaiah and Daniel. But many secular history books, like *The Works of Josephus*,[1] tell the story of the years between the testaments. One reason to investigate this time period is to understand why the Jewish people of the New Testament thought and acted differently than the Jewish people of the Old Testament. It was during this time in history that the Pharisees and Sadducees, leaders of the Law, arose. The silent years show what caused the Jews to be so concerned with following the Law.

To understand the message of the New Testament, we must remember its purpose is to show who Jesus Christ, Our Savior, is. The New Testament begins like the Old Testament with books of history. The books of history include the four gospels, which are Matthew, Mark, Luke, and John, with the final book of history being the book of Acts. The four Gospels describe the life of Christ from four different perspectives, and the book of Acts shares the story of how the *Gospel*, the "good news" of Jesus Christ,[2] was spread throughout the world. Jesus gave this command in the great commission right before he ascended into Heaven. "All authority in heaven and on earth has been given to me. Therefore go and make disciples of all nations, baptizing them in the name of the Father and of the Son and of the Holy Spirit, and teaching them to obey everything I have commanded you. And surely I am with you always, to the very end of the age" (Matt. 28:18–20). Acts introduces us to the first missionaries who left the comforts of their family and friends behind to share the Gospel with the world.

Following the books of history are twenty-one books of letters. To better understand their purpose, it is advantageous to study the book of Acts. They were to encourage the churches to hold fast to the Gospel. Out of the four reasons that we previously discussed concerning why God gave us the Bible, the letters tell us what God expects from us—how we are to love Him and love others.

The first thirteen letters were written by Paul. Starting with Romans through 2 Thessalonians, these letters were written to different churches that Paul visited to encourage them how to live a godly life. 1 and 2 Timothy, Titus, and Philemon are letters Paul wrote to individuals concerning how to be leaders in the church and how to treat fellow Christians. The remaining letters are considered the general letters written by various authors including James, Peter, John, Jude, and the unknown author of Hebrews. These letters give us hope, give warnings about false teachers, and emphasize the importance of Jesus as our Lord and Savior.

Finally, Revelation, the final book of the Bible, is a book of prophecy. *Revelation* means "an uncovering, a removal of the veil, a disclosure of what was previously unknown."[3] For this reason, the book of Revelation is also called "apocalyptic." It describes future events pertaining to the church and the judgment of mankind.

---

[1] Josephus, Flavius, and William Whiston. *The Works of Josephus: Complete and Unabridged*. New Updated ed. Peabody, Mass.: Hendrickson Publishers, 1987.

[2] Butler, Trent C. "Gospel" In *Holman Bible Dictionary: With Summary Definitions and Explanatory Articles on Every Bible Subject, Introductions and Teaching Outlines for Each Bible Book, In–depth Theological Articles,*

plus Internal Maps, Charts, Illustrations, Scale Reconstruction Drawings, Archaeological Photos, and Atlas. Nashville, Tenn.: Holman Bible Publishers, 1991.

3   Ibid, "Revelation."

Chapter 2

Building the Skeleton

*Your word is a lamp to my feet
and a light for my path*
(Psalm 119:105).

After learning the basics, it is time to start building a skeleton of the Bible. The word *skeleton* refers to the basic foundation of information. In the Bible, the basic foundation is the twelve historical periods. Once you understand and can recognize the twelve historical periods, any study or sermon can be placed on the skeleton to reveal a clearer picture. The skeleton connects the stories and truths of the Bible together to help better understand God's message. Without the skeleton, the stories and information learned become just bits and pieces that seem to have no apparent connection.

In addition to "Chart 1: Divisions of the Books of the Bible," there are two additional charts located in the appendix that will help visualize what we are discussing. "Chart 2: Books of the Bible by Historical Period" (see page 109) will help us begin to develop a skeleton by connecting the books to the twelve historical periods. Down the center of the chart the historical periods are listed. The column on the left lists the seventeen books of history, each paired with the time period discussed within their pages. The remaining forty-nine books of the Bible are listed in the far right column.

These books, which include the humanities, prophecy, and letters, are displayed to show how they fit into the time periods to enhance the story of the Bible. To develop the skeleton of the Bible, it is not necessary to discuss them, but later, in further Bible studies, they will be invaluable in adding meat to the skeleton. Therefore, since the basic message of the Bible is found in the history books, we will concentrate on them.

"Chart 3: Bible Chronological History Chart" (see page 110-111) shows the chronological order of events that occurred during the historical periods of the Bible. On the left side of the page, the twelve periods are listed. Down the center of the chart is a diagram of the major events that transpired. Starting at the top of the chart at "The Creation," follow the diagram down through the "Early Race of Mankind," the "Early Development of Israel," and through the leadership of Moses and Joshua. The "12 Men and a Woman" refer to the period of the Judges. Further down, you come to the three kings, who reigned during the time of "The Kingdom of Israel": Saul, David, and Solomon. From there, the line splits because after the death of King Solomon, the kingdom divided into the Southern Kingdom of Judah and the Northern Kingdom of Israel. Going to the right, follow the line down through the chronological order of the Northern Kingdom of Israel. Outside the vertical line in the diagram are listed the kings of the Northern Kingdom of Israel with the number of years they reigned. Notice that the Northern Kingdom of Israel had multiple dynasties that ruled. When you follow the chronological order down to the end of the line, it turns to the right and continues off the page. This shows Assyria defeated the Northern Kingdom of Israel and took them away into captivity. There is no mention in the Bible of the Northern Kingdom as a nation again. Back at the split under King Solomon, going to the left, follow the line down through the chronological order of the Southern Kingdom of Judah. As with the Northern Kingdom of Israel, the kings are listed with the years that each reigned, but notice that there was no change in the dynasty that ruled. The first king, Rehoboam, was the son of Solomon. Every king that followed in the Southern Kingdom was a direct descendent of King David. As God had promised, the line of David remained on the throne (2 Sam. 7:16). Inside the vertical lines are double-underlined names of prophets, who prophesized to the nations the impending judgment of God if the nation did not repent. Notice the names closest to the lines are the prophets of the respected kingdoms. The three prophets listed down the middle were prophets to other nations, and each is listed at the approximate time of their prophecy. Following the line of the Southern Kingdom of Judah, notice that it takes a sharp turn to the left when the Southern Kingdom of Judah was carried away into Babylonian captivity. During this time, Daniel and Ezekiel were prophets to the Judeans, reminding the people that God was with them and would eventually lead them out of captivity. This fulfilled promise is noted when the line returns to the right, signifying the return of a remnant of Judeans back to Jerusalem. The line then continues downward through "The Restoration of Israel" with the men in leadership on the left and the prophets on the right. This line takes you into the New Testament, beginning with "The Life of Christ" to "The Establishment of the Early Church" and beyond. The most significant part of the diagram is the straight line down the center from "The Garden" to "The Cross." This represents God's plan that had no deviation. No matter what man chose to do, God's plan remained constant. The Bible says, "Many are the plans in a man's heart, but it is the LORD's purpose that prevails" (Prov. 19:21). The introduction of sin in the Garden sent God's love straight to the cross. This is my most treasured chart that I keep folded in my Bible for reference when I start a new study. In one glance, I can look and see where the new area of study fits in the chronological order and understand what is happening during that period.

    Charts 2 and 3 will be invaluable through the remainder of this book. The rest of this chapter is a brief overview of the historical periods. The final chapter digs deeper into the content.

Sandra Betz

CONNECTING THE HISTORICAL PERIODS OF THE BIBLE

I. Creation to Abraham

This period of history is recorded in the first eleven chapters of Genesis. Here, God is dealing with the human race, beginning with Adam and taking us to the calling of Abram. How long is this period of time? It is as long as the remaining historical periods of the Bible combined or more.

Starting in Genesis 1–2, the great events of this period begin with the creation of the universe and man. God created all things perfect. We know this because the Bible says, "His (God's) works are perfect" (Deut. 32:4). The Bible also tells us that God had fellowship with man in the Garden; He took walks with him (Gen. 3:8). Can you imagine walking with God on a beautiful sunny afternoon!? I have no doubt Adam and Eve treasured many walks with God. But, this honor came with responsibility. Adam was commanded to take care of the Garden and work it, along with the specific command to not eat from the Tree of Knowledge of Good and Evil (Gen. 2:15–17). Understand, all other plants and trees were given to Adam except for this special tree (Gen. 1:30; 2:16–17). Just like a parent's rules are not to deprive but to protect their children so are God's rules. And just like children, they thought they knew what was best for them, so they chose to eat from the forbidden tree. Sin was birthed into the world by their rebellious act (1 Cor. 15:21–22). And, just like a parent, God had to deliver consequences. The consequences for Adam and Eve were great. No more walks in the Garden with God. That intimate relationship was broken. They had to be sent out of the Garden to be protected from eating from the Tree of Life that would cause them to live eternally in their sin (Gen. 3:22). If they remained in sin, then they would never be able to return back into fellowship with God.

But God loved man and did not want to remain separated from him. A plan was revealed to bring man back into relationship, a plan of salvation (Gen. 3:15; Jn. 3:16). Herein lies the wonderful love God has for all mankind. The journey to the cross begins as Adam and Eve are expelled from the garden. You might wonder why God took so long for His plan to be fulfilled. Only God knows that answer, but I believe that the Bible shows us that mankind had to understand why we needed a savior and to have some appreciation for how much God loves us. We had to recognize that we need Him. Hence, the journey to the cross.

After Adam and Eve were expelled from the Garden, sin continued. Cain, the son of Adam, murdered his brother Abel revealing more of the sinfulness of man (Gen. 4:8). At the end of the chapter, God's mercy was revealed with the birth of Seth. Through his line several thousand years later, Jesus, our Savior, was born (Luke 3:23–37). Even before the beginning of creation, God was prepared. The plans for the coming of a savior were already in place (Titus 1:2).

The flood (Gen. 6–8) is the next event recorded where the sinfulness of man became even more apparent. Man had failed to show that through his own ability he could re-establish a relationship with God. Instead, the wickedness of man increased. God was grieved He had made man. He told Noah, "I am going to put an end to all people, for the earth is filled with violence because of them. I am surely going to destroy both them and the earth" (Gen. 6:13). But because of His grace and mercy, God chose to save Noah and his family. After the flood, God then established a covenant with Noah and his descendants to replace the covenant made with Adam (Gen. 9:1–17). Unfortunately, this second beginning, even though it was fathered by a righteous man (Gen. 6:9), also failed. God was showing us that no matter how righteous we are, we need God's perfect righteousness to have a relationship with Him.

The final event recorded during this historical period shows the complete depravity of man. After the flood, God had commanded the people to scatter and multiply (Gen. 9:1). In Genesis 11, we find the story of the Tower of Babel. Within only a couple hundred years after the flood, man was trying to build a tower to the heavens, where he could make a name for himself "and not be scattered over the face of the whole earth" (Gen. 11:4). As a consequence of this disobedience, God caused the confusion of languages (Gen. 11:6–7). Without the ability to communicate, the people were unable to work on the tower together. They were forced to scatter over all the earth as God had commanded them to do initially (Gen. 11:8–9). At this point, we begin to realize the Old Testament is a "school teacher" to show us our need for a savior. Repeatedly, man had failed in restoring the relationship with God. Starting with a man named Abram, God began to grow a nation unto himself. As God ruled and led, His People would show the world what God was like and what God demanded.

II. Abraham to Moses

The second period of history is recorded in Genesis 12–50. It is noted as the time from Abraham to Moses. The stories within these pages center on the growing family of Abram. Because God still desired a relationship with man, He chose Abram to be the father of Israel, the nation that from its descendants would become the provision for sin. Approximately 2000 years after Abram lived, a savior was born to this nation. He would make it possible for all mankind to again have a close and intimate relationship with the One True God. But until then, this nation was chosen to show the world who God is and what He is like.

There are five great events of this time period. We begin with the call of God to Abram while he was in Ur of the Chaldeans in Mesopotamia (Acts 7:2–3). In Genesis 12:1–3, the Scripture records:

> *The LORD had said to Abram, "Leave your country, your people and your father's household and go to the land I will show you.*

> *"I will make you into a great nation*
>   *and I will bless you;*
> *I will make your name great,*
>   *and you will be a blessing.*
> *I will bless those who bless you,*
>   *and whoever curses you I will curse;*
> *and all peoples on earth*
>   *will be blessed through you."*

Verse 4 tells us Abram responded to the call. "So Abram left, as the LORD had told him." Abram obeyed and the world was blessed. Later, when God confirmed His covenant with Abram, He changed Abram's name to Abraham because God wanted Him to be recognized as the father of His nation (Gen. 17:4–5).

The next three great events included in this time period tell of the growing family of Abraham. The story of Isaac, Abraham's son, begins in Genesis 21. The story of Isaac's son, Jacob, is recorded in Genesis 25–50. God renewed with each one of these Patriarchs the covenant He made with Abraham to become a great nation that would bless the world.

The final great event is the story of Jacob's twelve sons. Joseph is the primary focus because God used him to save the family of Jacob from a great famine by bringing them into the land of Egypt. This inevitably saved the future generations of Abraham from extinction. The story of Joseph shows God's hand over His people, protecting them through history. Because Joseph is discussed more than any of the other sons of Jacob, many people assume that Jesus came from the line of Joseph, but it is important to note that Jesus the Messiah did not come through Joseph's line. Instead, the Messiah came through the line of Judah, who was Jacob's fourth son (Matt. 1:2–3). But, each son was significant because from their lineage came the twelve tribes of Israel.

III. The Exodus and the Years of Wandering

Between the closing chapter of Genesis and the opening verse of Exodus, Jacob's family had multiplied (Ex. 1:6–7, 9). As the Hebrews, the descendants of Jacob (Gen. 14:13), multiplied, the Egyptians became fearful of their numbers and enslaved them. The Israelites reacted by crying out to God for help. God heard their cry and raised up Moses to deliver His people out of Egypt. After a series of plagues orchestrated by God, Pharaoh allowed the Israelites to leave. By God's direction, Moses led them across the Red Sea, through the wilderness, and to the land of Canaan, also known as the Promised Land. When they arrived, Moses sent in spies to search out the territory, but after hearing some of the reports, the people were afraid to trust God with the challenges of the land and chose not to enter. Because of their disobedience and because they did not trust God, God sentenced the Israelites to roam the desert for forty years before they could enter the land of promise (Num. 32:13). During that time, all the adults died except for Joshua and Caleb, who had trusted God (Num. 14:29–30). These years are found in the books of Exodus, Leviticus, Numbers, and Deuteronomy.

IV. The Conquest of Canaan

The book of Joshua tells the story of a brief but brilliant era of the Israelites entering the Promised Land after forty years of wandering in the desert. After the death of Moses, Joshua became the military leader to command and lead the people. After traveling dry-shod over the Jordan River, they soon pierced the center of the land with the conquest of Jericho. From there, the Israelites conquered many of the people of the south before they headed north in their continued invasion of the land. By a series of decisive campaigns, they defeated many of the inhabitants.

After the Israelites' initial assault on the land, Joshua, under God's leadership, divided the land among the twelve tribes and commanded each tribe to individually carry forward the conquest until they were in full possession of their allotment. [Note: The Levites were to be spread throughout the other tribes. Their portion was not land but their service to God (Josh. 18:7).] Unfortunately, the tribes did not fully take the land. Instead, the Bible records times when they befriended or enslaved the people of the land instead of subduing them (Judg. 1:28). This disobedience led to the years of failure and defeat during the time of the Judges that Joshua had warned the people about before his death (Josh. 23:12–13).

V. The Judges

After the glorious days of Joshua came the mournful days of the Judges. The books of Judges and Ruth record the stories from this period. Israel was a theocracy, a nation where God was the sovereign ruler. But, the people rebelled against God's authority. So, instead of becoming a strong nation with God's leadership, Israel became a nation of repeated failure and defeat. These years were marked by a continuous cycle of peace, then disobedience, then oppression, then crying out to God, and then deliverance. When the people cried out to God, they would rally at Shiloh where the Tabernacle had been set up (Josh. 18:1). Each time God delivered the nation out of oppression, He would raise up a judge to lead His people (Judg. 2:11–23). This cycle of rebellion and repentance continued until Saul became king of Israel.

VI. The Kingdom of Israel

This period of history is recorded in 1 and 2 Samuel, 1 Kings 1–11, 1 Chronicles, and 2 Chronicles 1–9. It begins with the introduction of Samuel, the last judge of the Israelites (1 Sam. 7:15). When Samuel was old, the Israelites cried out to him for an earthly king (1 Sam. 8:4–5). They wanted a king like the other nations. God told Samuel to listen to them, but told him to warn the people of the challenges of an earthly king (1 Sam. 8:9–18). The people refused to listen. God respected the Israelites' desire and commanded Samuel to anoint Saul as the first king of Israel (1 Sam. 9:15–17). The tribes of Israel stood united as one kingdom through the reigns of three kings: Saul, David, and Solomon.

After Saul reigned forty years (Acts 13:21), David was anointed king (1 Sam. 16:12–13). The Bible says that he was a man after God's own heart (1 Sam. 13:14). He loved God so much that he wanted to build a permanent temple where God could dwell among men, but God had other plans (1 Chron. 22:7–10). God's command for David was to conquer the land the Israelites had not yet brought under submission. God promised David that his son, Solomon, would build the Temple (2 Sam. 7:12–13). More importantly, God made an everlasting covenant with David: "Your house and your kingdom will endure forever before me; your throne will be established forever" (2 Sam. 7:16). This promise was fulfilled in the lineage of David with the birth, death, and resurrection of Jesus Christ (Mt. 1:1; 1 Cor. 15:4; Rev. 5:8–14).

The reign of Solomon was considered "The Golden Age" of Israel's history when Israel attained its highest glory. It was a time of peace (1 Kings 4:24). With the government firmly established, Israel's borders were pushed to the Nile in one direction and to the Euphrates in the other. Unfortunately, Solomon's downfall was that he married women from other nations; they influenced him to worship other gods. Because of these sinful acts, God told Solomon that He would tear away part of the kingdom, but this would not occur until after Solomon's death (1 Kings 11:11–13).

VII. The Divided Kingdom

Solomon's son, Rehoboam, took the throne after Solomon's death. He was a tyrant who made the people work even harder than they did during the time of the construction of God's Temple and Solomon's palace (1 Kings 12:11). Ten of the twelve tribes rebelled against the harsh treatment and chose Jeroboam to lead in the rebellion. This uprising was so great that it ripped apart the kingdom. This left the Southern Kingdom of Judah with Rehoboam as king and the Northern Kingdom of Israel (1 Kings 12:23) with Jeroboam as king (1 Kings 12:20).

The Temple gave the Southern Kingdom a place to continue to worship God and maintain a relationship with Him through sacrifice. But in the Northern Kingdom, there was no place to meet with God. Without the Temple, there was no place to make sacrifices. Jeroboam did not want the people to return to the Temple in the Southern Kingdom of Judah because he feared he would lose his position (1 Kings 12:26–27). The Bible says that Jeroboam instead constructed an altar in the Northern Kingdom of Israel for worship. "After seeking advice, the king (Jeroboam) made two golden calves. He said to the people, 'It is too much for you to go up to Jerusalem. Here are your gods, O Israel, who brought you up out of Egypt'" (1 Kings 12:28). Disobedience to God's commands pulled the Northern Kingdom away from God and His laws. There was little to remind them of where they had been and *who* had delivered them. Eventually, the Northern Kingdom of Israel was taken away into captivity by Assyria and was never mentioned again in the Bible as a nation. Because they did not obey God, they lost their identity and their direction. But God's plan continued through the Southern Kingdom of Judah. As we will see, the remnant of Israel was saved through the line of Judah. This period of the Divided Kingdom is recorded in 1 Kings 12–22, 2 Kings 1–17, and 2 Chronicles 10–31.

VIII. The Southern Kingdom of Judah Alone

After the Northern Kingdom was led away into captivity, the Southern Kingdom stood alone. Judah had Jerusalem! The Temple constantly reminded the people of who God is and aided the nation in reminding them of where they had been. God sent prophets to warn the Judeans (people of Judah; 1 Chron. 4:18) that if they did not obey His commands, God would allow them to be carried away into captivity just like the people of the Northern Kingdom. But in spite of God's warnings and in spite of the presence of the Temple, the Southern Kingdom of Judah eventually went deeper and deeper into sin and idolatry. This period can be found in 2 Kings 18–24:9 and 2 Chronicles 32–36:9.

IX. The Captivity of Judah

Because of the Southern Kingdom of Judah's continued disobedience, God's righteousness forced Him to bring the people of Judah under judgment. To do this, God raised up King Nebuchadnezzar of Babylon to conquer the Southern Kingdom of Judah and bring them under submission (2 Chron. 36:16–17). During the siege, Jerusalem was destroyed and the Temple was devastated. The Bible says, "They (Babylonians) set fire to God's Temple and broke down the wall of Jerusalem; they burned all the palaces and destroyed everything of value there" (2 Chron. 36:19; see 2 Kings 25:8–10). After Nebuchadnezzar had control over the land, he ordered a majority of the captives taken to Babylon, where they became servants to the people of Babylon (2 Chron. 36:20). Without their land and without the Temple to communicate with God, they were isolated and weakened as a nation. God's chosen people had marched dry-shod over the Jordan River in triumph but now marched away in chains. The people from Judah would remain in Babylon captivity for the next seventy years just as Jeremiah had prophesied (2 Chron.

36:20–21; Jer. 29:10). This story is recorded in 2 Kings 24:10–25:30, 2 Chronicles 36:10–23, and in the book of Daniel.

X. The Restoration of Israel

Just as the time of the captivity of Judah showed God's righteousness, the time of the restoration revealed His grace. His judgment of Judah was to bring them to repentance and to return them to covenant with Him. This was accomplished by the remnant of Israel returning to rebuild Jerusalem and the Temple during the Mede-Persian captivity.

In just one night, the Mede-Persians invaded and conquered the Babylonian Empire, becoming the new masters of the enslaved Judeans (Dan. 5:30–31). Unlike the Babylonians, the Mede-Persians did not demand their servitude. Instead, Cyrus, King of Persia, upon accession to the throne, issued a decree permitting the people of God to return and rebuild their city and the Temple (Ezra 1:2–5). Even though they were allowed to return to Jerusalem, they remained under the authority of the Mede-Persian Empire. Ezra, a teacher of the Scriptures, returned to Jerusalem years after the Temple was built to help with the restoration of the people's hearts (Ezra 7). Later, Nehemiah arrived to encourage the people to continue building the wall around the city (Neh. 2:17–18). During this period in history is when God's people were first called "Jews" (Ezra 4:12). These events are recorded in the books of Ezra, Nehemiah, Esther, and Daniel.

Between the Testaments

The Old Testament closes with the remnant of the nation of Israel restoring the city of Jerusalem and God's Temple. The next four hundred years of history between the Old and New Testaments are barely mentioned in the Bible. But from secular writings, we learn that the Jews passed through various stages and experiences that affected many of their customs and even their language.

After the Babylonian captivity, the Jews feared the consequences of falling out of favor with God and returning to bondage. Many became obsessed about their commitment in following God's written laws to the letter. Over time, the oral law, "the authoritative interpretation of the Written Law,"[1] was pushed by a religious sect called the Pharisees. They wanted to make sure every situation brought obedience. Sadly, the Pharisees and other Jewish leaders' attitude toward the Law only caused them to be chained to the Law. They became so obsessed with obedience that they forgot the purpose of the Law, which was to maintain a relationship with God. During these years the Pharisees and Sadducees, another religious sect, became the leading factions of the Jewish community that pushed for the obedience of the Law.[2]

XI. Life of Christ

After the long silent years between the testaments, the voice of God was again heard. John the Baptist burst onto the beginning pages of the New Testament with the message of repentance. He preached that the coming of the Messiah was at hand. "Repent, for the kingdom of heaven is near" (Matt. 3:2). The promise of a savior that was first made in the Garden (Gen. 3:15) and repeated with increasing clarity and emphasis throughout the Old Testament was fulfilled with the coming of Jesus Christ. The Messiah came, manifested Himself, was rejected, and was crucified. Then Jesus the Messiah, the Son of God, rose from the grave to reign with His Father forever. With His life, death, and resurrection, Jesus Christ became our provision for sin.

God wanted us to know His Son, our Savior, so He had four men write about Jesus Christ through four different perspectives. These different viewpoints of Christ are found in the four Gospels: Matthew, Mark, Luke, and John. The term *Gospel* initially was used to refer to the message of salvation through Jesus Christ but was later accepted to reference these four documents.[3] Collectively, these books not only give us a written documentation about Jesus's life but show us through His life who God is. Each shows a different perspective of Jesus and why God's Son is the only way to the Father.

The first book in the New Testament is the Gospel according to Matthew. Matthew was one of the twelve apostles of Christ. The purpose of his writing was to show the Jews that Jesus is King, the Messiah. Matthew begins by affirming Jesus's line of royalty through Joseph, his earthly adopted father, back to Abraham, the father of the Israelites (Matt. 1:1). Throughout the text, Matthew reinforces his message by comparing Old Testament prophecy of the coming of the Messiah with the actual life of Christ to emphasize his point that Jesus is the Savior, whom the Jews had awaited the arrival of for centuries. For example, Matthew references Micah 5:2, "But you, Bethlehem, in the land of Judah, are by no means least among the rulers of Judah; for out of you will come a ruler who will be the shepherd of my people Israel" (Matt. 2:6). The book of Matthew contains more references to fulfilled prophecies relating to the Messiah than any of the other three Gospel accounts.

The book of Mark portrays Jesus as the suffering servant. "Sitting down, Jesus called the Twelve and said, 'If anyone wants to be first, he must be the very last, and the servant of all'" (Mark 9:35). From 1 Peter 5:13 and the early church fathers, Papias, and Eusebius, we learn that Mark was a follower of Peter and recorded experiences that Peter had with Jesus.[4] Therefore, it is believed that Mark's words are Peter's testimony of his years with Jesus. Mark's chronological account is very matter of fact, containing little detail. His account is believed to have been used by the other synoptic Gospel writers as a template for their own manuscripts.[5] The books of Matthew, Mark, and Luke are referred to as the synoptic Gospels. The Zondervan Illustrated Bible Dictionary defines *synoptic* as "to see the whole together, to take a comprehensive view."[6] Comparing these three books shows that they all have similar content and verbiage. The fourth Gospel, the book of John, is distinctly different in its content because John's purpose was to show Jesus as the Son of God.[7] Therefore, John concentrated on the events of Jesus's ministry rather than on the events of his life.

The third Gospel writer, Luke, was a physician who traveled with Paul on his missionary journeys. The purpose of his writing was to show Jesus as fully man.[8] In doing so, he penned the most extensive description of Jesus's birth. He was the only Gospel writer to mention Jesus's presentation to the Lord at eight days of age (Luke 2:22–38) and Jesus's visit to the Temple with His family for the Feast of Passover at the age of twelve (Luke 2:41–50). These are life events that most Jewish children would have experienced. Concerning his teenage and young adult years, nothing is written, except that "Jesus grew in wisdom and stature, and in favor with God and men" (Luke 2:52). The lack of information about His upbringing is a good example that God had written in the Scriptures what He knew we needed to know. Before Luke discusses Jesus's years of ministry, he records Jesus's genealogy through his mother, Mary, all the way back to Adam, emphasizing Jesus as a member of mankind (Luke 3:23–38). Luke emphasized the basic human needs of Jesus, such as the need for food and the need for rest. He further emphasized Jesus's suffering as a man as He endured the arrest, the trials, and finally the crucifixion.

John, the writer of the final Gospel, was most likely the youngest disciple of Jesus. From his very first words, he wanted us to recognize Jesus as deity. "In the beginning was the Word, and the Word was with God, and the Word was God. He was with God in the beginning" (John 1:1–2). Here, John tells us that Jesus is the Word and reveals the presence of Jesus with God at the beginning of creation. This reference to Jesus as the Word is best explained in John 12:49–50 when Jesus said, "For I did not speak of my own accord, but the Father who sent me commanded me what to say and how to say it. I know that his command leads to eternal life. So whatever I say is just what the Father has told me to say." Jesus's words were God's Words. He was God's direct messenger from Heaven to man. John wrote to tell us that God loves us. One of the most well-known and memorized verses in the Bible comes from his book. "For God so loved the world that he gave his one and only Son, that whoever believes in him shall not perish but have eternal life" (John 3:16). This reveals God's love is personal. In the time John spent with Jesus, he realized that God loves each of us individually. I would not be surprised if John had read the words of David found in the book of Psalms, "Keep me as the apple of your eye" (Ps. 17:8). After Jesus died on the cross, John recognized Jesus died for each of us individually because He wanted a relationship with each of us individually.

I am so thankful that God allowed these four men to write about our Savior. The stories teach us about His life and in turn, give us life.

XII. The Establishment of the Early Church

The final book of history found in the Bible is Acts which covers the Establishment of the Early Church. It begins with the ascension of Jesus to heaven. But before being taken up, Jesus instructed His disciples to wait for the gift of the Holy Spirit, who would empower them to be witnesses to all peoples (Acts 1:4–5). Chapter 2 of Acts records the coming of the Spirit at Pentecost (Acts 2:1–13). After the anointing of the Holy Spirit, Peter preached a powerful sermon and many believed and became part of the early church (Acts 2:14–36). Soon, persecution came which spread the Gospel beyond the walls of Jerusalem. The most dramatic conversion told in the pages of Acts is the transformation of Saul. Known for his murderous threats to the disciples, he was on his way to Damascus to imprison more Christians when the glorified Jesus stopped him in his tracks (Acts 9:1–19). Saul, later known as Paul, was transformed that day from a zealous Pharisee (Phil. 3:4–6) to a humble, unstoppable witness for Christ (Phil. 3:13–14). The second half of Acts records mainly the spread of the Gospel to the Gentiles through Paul's missionary journeys.

Following Acts is the New Testament letters (see page 108). These letters expand upon the history found in Acts. To have a clear understanding of the messages of the letters, Acts must be studied, and in turn, to better understand the history recorded in Acts, the letters must be studied.

---

[1] Friedman, Theodore. "Oral Law." Http://www.jewishvirtuallibrary.org. Accessed March 26, 2015. http://www.jewishvirtuallibrary.org/jsource/judaica/ejud_0002_0015_0_15166.html

[2] Butler, Trent C. "Jewish Parties in the New Testament" In *Holman Bible Dictionary: With Summary Definitions and Explanatory Articles on Every*

3   Ibid, "Gospel."
4   Just SJ, Felix. "Eusebius, Ecclesiastical History 3 – On the Gospel Authorship." Http://catholic–resources.org – On the Gospel Authorship. November 11, 2006. Accessed March 23, 2015. http://catholic–resources.org/Bible/Eusebius_Gospels.htm
5   Walvoord, John F., and Roy B. Zuck, eds. *The Bible Knowledge Commentary: An Exposition of the Scriptures.* New Testament ed. Colorado Springs, Colo.: Cook Communications Ministries, 2004. 96–97.
6   Douglas, J.D., and Merrill C. Tenney. "Synoptic" In *Zondervan Illustrated Bible Dictionary: The Most Accurate and Comprehensive One–volume Bible Dictionary Available.* Grand Rapids, Mich.: Zondervan, 1987.
7   Walvoord, John F., and Roy B. Zuck, eds. *The Bible Knowledge Commentary: An Exposition of the Scriptures.* New Testament ed. Colorado Springs, Colo.: Cook Communications Ministries, 2004. 268.
8   Ibid, 199.

Bible Subject, Introductions and Teaching Outlines for Each Bible Book, In–depth Theological Articles, plus Internal Maps, Charts, Illustrations, Scale Reconstruction Drawings, Archaeological Photos, and Atlas. Nashville, TN: Holman Bible Publishers, 1991.

Chapter 3

Adding Meat to the Skeleton

*The fear of the LORD is the beginning of wisdom;
all who follow his precepts have good understanding.
To him belongs eternal praise*
(Psalm 111:10).

In Chapter 2, we successfully constructed a basic foundation of the Bible. This gave us a simple outline or a skeleton of God's Word. Examining this skeleton, we can begin to see God's message weaved through Scripture. God loves us and desires to have a relationship with us. Repeatedly throughout history, God has reached down to mankind and called us to Him. We do not deserve to be called, but God's love and His compassion brings forth His mercy and His grace.

In this final chapter, we strengthen the structure by adding detail or meat to each historical period. This will help form a solid foundation, which will be helpful later when individually studying the stories and truths in the different periods.

The Old Testament

As you read and study the Old Testament, look for the recurring theme of man's inability to remain consistently in God's favor. God gave the Law to Moses for man to live by, but man was easily distracted. Idols and worldly pleasures wooed his eyes and ears to other things besides God. Temporary sacrificial offerings and laws were put in place by God to bring man back into a relationship with Him. But, it is not until the New Testament time that God intervened on our behalf and sent His Son to fulfill what man could not. To understand what Jesus Christ has done for us, we have to first understand what man did without Him. Thus, God gave us the story of the Old Testament.

I. Creation to Abraham

A. Creation

The Bible begins with God. Genesis 1:1 states, "God created the heavens and the earth." There is no attempt to prove His existence. God was and God is. If we desire to truly understand God's message to us and His love for us, we must first accept that He is God and that He was there at the beginning. "Trust in the LORD with all your heart and lean not on your own understanding; in all your ways acknowledge him, and he will make your paths straight" (Prov. 3:5–6). Trusting in God is the only way to know Him. We must accept the truth of Genesis 1:1 to be able to hear the message of the Bible.

From the first word, the Bible states that God did it! God spoke creation into being (Gen. 1:3). Therefore, the heavens and the earth belong to Him! Not only does the heavens and the earth belong to Him, but we belong to Him because He created us (Gen. 1:27). Thankfully, He is a God of love (1 John 4:8). So, if we are His, we do not need to fear His wrath. Instead, we know that in all things He has our best interest in mind.

God prepared a dwelling place for mankind. For six days, He spoke creation into existence. When a gardener decides to grow a crop, he does not go into an unprepared field and throw the seed. Instead, he chooses the land wisely and then begins the process of preparing the field where the seed can be sown in the best place the land has to offer for the best growth possible. After the field is properly prepared, the farmer then plants the seeds. We find the same careful preparation in God creating man. The first five days prepared an environment for His prize creation. Each day God added something new and exciting, but we find ourselves drawn to day six for the culmination of creation. On day six, the preparations were completed. The time had come. The Bible says, "God created man in His own image" and placed him in the Garden (Gen. 1:27). God gave him a part of Himself when He breathed His own breath of life into man (Gen. 2:7). Not only did God create man, but He formed him. His actions show a personal involvement. Beth Moore stated in her study *Believing God*, "I believe God wanted to do more than speak us into existence. I think He wanted to get His hands involved… God formed our bodies with His very own hands. You might even say that God was willing to get His hands dusty."[1] This sets man apart from all creation. To no other part of creation did God give so much of Himself. This emphasizes His desire to know us and to become personally involved in our lives.

As a loving Creator, God made sure that man had everything he needed. In the second chapter of Genesis, verse 18, He made woman. "The LORD God said, 'It is not good for the man to be alone. I will make a helper suitable for him.'" From the very beginning, God's perfect plan was for one man and one woman to marry. He knew this would be man's perfect companion. Adam had a place to live, a companion to live with, and a God who loved him. Adam had everything he needed.

At the end of the sixth day, we read, "God saw all that he had made, and it was very good" (Gen. 1:31). Creation was complete. When the sun rose on the seventh day, God set it apart as a day of rest from all that He had done (Gen. 2:3). If God felt the need to rest from His work, then it must be surmised that we need our rest. We need a day to reflect on the work that we have done and remember whose we are. In the Old Testament, God chose the Sabbath, Saturday, as a day of rest. In the New Testament, the apostles seem to have been led to gather together on Sunday because it was the day on which the Lord rose from the grave, called the "Lord's Day" (Rev. 1:10). What is important is that we set aside a day each week to rest our body and renew our heart and mind to God. If we put aside one day a week for renewal, then the rest of the week we will be more focused on Him for guidance, and we will want to praise Him for who He is.

Before we close the pages on creation, consider that the days of God might not be our own 24-hour days. Psalms 90:4 states, "For a thousand years in your sight are like a day that has just gone by, or like a watch in the night." We cannot be sure how long it took God to create the universe. God could have taken six 24-hour days, or His days could have been thousands of our days. The time is not important. What is important is that God did it. And it belongs to Him.

God made the universe perfect. He made man *innocent*, "without sin but untested."[2] He gave man all that he would need. At this point, He could have left man alone and worked on another project. But instead, after all that God had done, He sealed His love for man by fellowshipping with him. Life was perfect for Adam and Eve. God and man had a relationship. Nothing could separate them but man himself. Unfortunately, Adam and Eve did just that.

B. The Fall

God had created angels to serve Him (Neh. 9:6), but He had not created a being that could choose to serve and fellowship with Him. So, God created man for this purpose. It is important to understand that when God created Adam and Eve, they did not know good and evil (Gen. 3:7). They were in innocence. God cared for them and guided them toward good. But for man to be able to choose to serve Him, God had to give man the gift of choice. In Genesis 2, God made a covenant with Adam. It involved one simple rule. "And the LORD God commanded the man, 'You are free to eat from any tree in the garden; but you must not eat from the tree of the knowledge of good and evil, for when you eat of it you will surely die'" (Gen. 2:16–17). God gave man a choice. Trust and obey me or die. Once they chose to eat from this tree, they became aware of sin, of its condemnation, and of its effect on their relationship with God. This became apparent when they hid from God (Gen. 3:8). God did not make this prohibition because He was trying to keep something from Adam. Instead, God was trying to protect Adam from being separated from Him.

So why did God allow this temptation? Without temptation, there is no choice. Choosing anything but God is choosing sin, and God cannot look upon sin because He is holy (Hab. 1:13). Because God is holy, He must judge sin (Heb. 4:12–13). When Adam and Eve chose to eat from the Tree of Knowledge (Gen. 3:6), they chose to disobey God. So for their protection, God sent them out of the garden and from His presence. "And the LORD God said, 'The man has now become like one of us, knowing good and evil. He must not be allowed to reach out his hand and take also from the tree of life and eat, and live forever.' So the LORD God banished him from the Garden of Eden to work the ground from which he had been taken" (Gen. 3:22–23). Evicting them from the garden was not only to remove them from God's presence but to prevent them from eating from the Tree of Life. If they had eaten from the Tree of Life, they would have lived forever in their sin and remained eternally out of fellowship with God. But God is the Great I Am (Exod. 3:14). Before the very foundation of the earth was laid, God knew that man would make a wrong choice. God was not surprised or shaken by man's disobedience. He did not have to race around in panic and try to figure out what to do. God was prepared. He had a plan.

There is no pause between the sin and the revelation of the provision. In Genesis 3:15, God is speaking to the serpent, which is Satan. "And I will put enmity between you and the woman, and between your offspring and hers; he will crush your head, and you will strike his heel." Let us break this down. "And I will put enmity between you and the woman and between your offspring and hers..." First, man and snakes generally are enemies. Man might be enticed by their beauty, but he must treat snakes with respect or be bitten. Second, the Bible tells us Satan was the most beautiful creature in heaven (Ezek. 28:12b–19). He rebelled against God and set out to destroy God's perfect plan for mankind. To this day, Satan tempts us to choose against God's plan. We must recognize Satan's enticing lure to sin so that we can avoid his snares. But there is more. The offspring of Eve is Jesus Christ. Jesus Christ was, is, and always will be an enemy of Satan. Here lies the provision, "...he will crush your head, and you will strike his heel." The "He" is Jesus Christ. When Christ died on the cross and rose from the grave, He defeated death; thereby crushing Satan. Christ's death was Satan's plan to separate God from man. Instead, Christ's death and resurrection brought hope, giving man an opportunity for a relationship with God. Finally, it is true that Satan did strike Jesus's heel; Christ did suffer on the cross, but Christ had the victory.

> *...Death has been swallowed up in victory.*
> *Where, O death, is your victory? Where, O death is your sting?*
> *The sting of death is sin, and the power of sin is the law.*
> *But thanks be to God! He gives us the victory*
> *through our Lord Jesus Christ*
> (1 Cor. 15:54b–57).

C. Cain and Abel

After Adam and Eve were sent out of the Garden, sin continued to develop and grow. The evidence is found in the story of Cain and Abel, two of Adam and Eve's sons (Gen. 4:1–2). Cain was the older sibling who worked the soil while Abel kept flocks. Scripture records the events when Cain and Abel brought an offering before the Lord. Cain's offering was not acceptable to the Lord, but the Lord favored Abel's. In Genesis 4:6–7, God gives Cain another opportunity to do what is right. "Then the LORD said to Cain, 'Why are you angry? Why is your face downcast? If you do what is right, will you not be accepted? But if you do not do what is right, sin is crouching at your door; it desires to have you, but you must master it.'" All that was required of Cain was to repent and "do what is right" (Gen. 4:7). Instead, Cain was angered and took his anger out on Abel. "Now Cain said to his brother Abel, 'Let's go out to the field.' And while they were in the field, Cain attacked his brother Abel and killed him" (Gen. 4:8). The murder of Abel illustrates the depth and depravity of sin and man's need for redemption. Because of his choice, Cain is cursed and banished as "a fugitive and a vagabond" (Gen. 4:12, KJV). God was prepared. In Genesis 4:25, God provided hope for mankind with the birth of Seth. Thousands of years later, through the line of Seth came the Savior who became the provision for sin.

D. The Flood

After Adam and Eve left the garden, the Bible tells us that man became filled with sin. The human race was warned of God's disapproval, but man did not respond. "The LORD saw how great man's wickedness on the earth had become, and that every inclination of the thoughts of his heart was only evil all the time. The LORD was grieved that he had made man on the earth, and his heart was filled with pain. So the LORD said, 'I will wipe mankind, whom I have created, from the face of the earth—men and animals, and creatures that move along the ground, and birds of the air—for I am grieved that I have made them'" (Gen. 6:5–7).

In the midst of a sinful mankind, God found one righteous man named Noah (Gen. 6:9). Understand, Noah was not perfect, but he recognized his sin and responded to God's calling. Unlike Noah, the rest of the human race did not respond even after warnings of God's displeasure with them. But Noah knew God and loved God. "But Noah found favor in the eyes of the LORD... Noah was a righteous man, blameless among the people of his time and he walked with God" (Gen. 6:8–9). God honors and blesses our devotion to Him. Noah and his family were spared because of Noah's obedience and God's mercy.

In Genesis 6–8, the Bible tells the story of the great flood. By God's direction, Noah built an ark that would carry his family and at least two of every living creature to safety (Gen. 7:1–2). The Bible says that water came up from the ground and fell from the heavens for forty days and nights (Gen. 7:11–12). After the waters had receded, the ark settled in the Ararat mountains (Gen. 8:4). When Noah and his family walked out of the ark, they were the beginning of a new race. All mankind born after the flood was descended from Noah. Noah had three sons: Shem, Ham and Japheth (Gen. 6:10). Why was there a death sentence for the rest of mankind? God was showing us that the consequence of sin is death and separation from God. We must have a repentant heart like Noah to escape death and separation from God. The story of the ark is a foreshadowing of God's provision of Jesus Christ for our salvation. Only those who entered the ark were saved. Only those who ask Christ to be their Lord and Savior are saved from the judgment and wrath of God (1 Pet. 3:19–21).

In Genesis 9:13, God promised never to allow a worldwide flood again. "I have set my rainbow in the clouds, and it will be the sign of the covenant between me and the earth." Never again will waters cover the earth destroying all life (Gen. 9:15). To this day, we often are reminded of this covenant after a rainstorm.

In Genesis 9:1, God told Noah's family to increase in number and fill the earth. The family did increase in number, but the generations did not fill the earth. Instead, mankind stayed together and settled in the land of Shinar, where they all spoke one language (Gen. 11:1–2). During this time, agriculture and technology grew. Written language began. Man used irrigation from the Tigris and Euphrates rivers to water their fields. At the same time, idolatry flourished. But again, man was turning from God. In the middle of the cities, tall ziggurats were built. These buildings were used to worship other gods. On the top of the ziggurats was where the people sacrificed to their gods.[3] The taller the ziggurat, the farther from the One True God the people became.

E. Confusion of Tongues

Mankind fell deeper into sin. The Bible says that the men of the earth attempted to build a tower up to heaven where they could make a name for themselves and not be spread out (Gen. 11:4). Man chose to appease his selfish desires instead of obeying God's commands. This mindset shows that the further we get away from God, the more centered we are on self. God saw man's disobedience and responded by coming down to man. God caused their language to be confused so that the people could no longer cooperate in their rebellion against Him (Gen. 11:7). They fell into confusion and began leaving the area of Babel and spreading throughout the world (Gen. 11:9). This dispersion was God's plan. What God had commanded was being carried out (Gen. 9:1). God was in control. His plan was still accomplished.

History tells us that the descendants of Noah's sons occupied different sections of the world. The people of Shem traveled to the area of Mesopotamia and the Arabian Peninsula and settled there.

From this group came the Israelites that Moses later led out of Egypt. Northern Africa became the settling place for the descendants of Ham. They would later be known as Africans. Japheth's descendants moved westward into Asia Minor and Europe and would eventually be called Europeans.[4]

Mankind had failed twice to regain a relationship with God. Each time sin had put a barrier between God and man. After showing mankind's failure, God began to call out a special people that He would work through to show the world who He is and His desire to have a relationship with them. Through this people came the provision for dealing with man's sin, enabling man to once again have a relationship with God. This would be the Son of God, Jesus Christ.

II. Abraham to Moses

A. Abraham and His Wanderings

In the land of Shinar was a city called Ur. In ancient times, the city was located close to where the Euphrates and Tigris met. Ur was a bustling metropolis known for its literary activity and its high level of commercial business, but it was blighted with idolatry and immorality (Josh. 24:2–4). From this city, God called out Abram to go to a land that He would show him. Through Abram's descendants, God grew the nation of Israel and claimed them as His own. The purpose of this nation was to reveal God to the world. In answering the Sanhedrin, "the highest Jewish council in the first century,"[5] charge of blasphemy in Acts 7, Stephen told the story of God calling out Abraham and making him the father of Israel. "Brothers and fathers, listen to me! The God of glory appeared to our father Abraham while he was still in Mesopotamia, before he lived in Haran. 'Leave your country and your people,' God said, 'and go to the land I will show you.' So he left the land of the Chaldeans and settled in Haran. After the death of his father, God sent him to this land where you are now living" (Acts 7:2–4).

Genesis 11:31–32 is where the story of Abram's journey to the Promised Land begins. Terah, Abram's father, took his family and left Ur to travel to Canaan. Scripture is not clear why Terah chose to leave, but God used Terah's plan to send Abram on his way. The family traveled up the Euphrates to Haran. Due to health or circumstance, Terah never left Haran. Abram tarried in Haran until the death of his father. There appears to be no chastisement of Abram for not going directly from Ur to Canaan. In fact, God probably honored Abram's decision to stay with his father because it was custom during this time for the oldest son to be responsible for his parents. Sometime after Terah's death, God renewed His call to Abram (Gen. 12:1–3). Abram took his family and his possessions as well as his nephew Lot and continued the journey to Canaan. God promised many wonderful things to Abram, and all Abram had to do was go. I have no doubt that it must have been difficult leaving familiar surroundings, but God went with him and supplied all his needs. Abram took the first step. God took the rest. "Abraham believed God, and it was credited to him as righteousness" (Rom. 4:3; see Gen. 15:6).

Once Abram arrived in Canaan, he never called any one place his home because God had not yet given the land to his people. During Abram's lifetime, it was only promised (Gen. 12:6–7). But Abram traveled throughout the land claiming it for God in faith by building altars and worshiping God everywhere he went.

One of the most remarkable truths found throughout Scripture is that God used people like you and me to do His work. Just like you and me, Abram did not always make the right choices. During a famine, Abram sojourned to Egypt (Gen. 12:10). Upon entering, Abram feared for his life. It was the custom of the land that any beautiful woman could be taken to Pharaoh to become part of his harem. If the woman was married, the husband was killed. Because Sarai, his wife, was beautiful, Abram had reason to be concerned.

Instead of depending on God for his safety, Abram chose to deceive Pharaoh. He told Sarai to tell everyone that he was her brother. So when Sarai was brought before Pharaoh, Abram was spared, but the troubles were just beginning. Shortly after Sarai entered the harem, Pharaoh's household was filled with disease. Pharaoh realized that Sarai must be the reason for the troubles, so he summoned Abram to his court. He questioned Abram why he did not tell him that Sarai was his wife. Then Pharaoh demanded that Abram take her and leave Egypt (Gen. 12:18–19). Abram immediately recognized his sin and traveled to Bethel to worship the Lord (Gen. 13:3–4). We need to be like Abram. When we stumble out of God's graces, we need to return to Him on bended knee with a repentant heart.

Scripture informs us that when Abram was sent out of Egypt, he left with everything Pharaoh had given him, including an abundance of livestock (Gen. 12:16, 20). In Genesis chapter 13, Abram and nephew Lot recognized that the land could not maintain all of their cattle and sheep. It therefore became necessary for them to separate. Abram allowed Lot to choose which land he preferred. Lot chose the beautiful, rich plain of the Jordan to the east, which was not wise because the land was near Sodom, where the men were evil against God (Gen. 13:13). But God was with Abram. He told him, "Lift up your eyes from where you are and look north and south, east and west. All the land that you see I will give to you and your offspring forever. I will make your offspring like the dust of the earth, so that if anyone could count the dust, then your offspring could be counted. Go, walk through the length and breadth of the land, for I am giving it to you" (Gen. 13:14–17). God richly blessed Abram because Abram trusted God. In praise and thanksgiving to God, Abram settled near the trees of Mamre in Hebron and built and altar to God (Gen. 13:18). Not only did Abram have a repentant heart, he had a thankful heart.

The Bible tells of two incidents where Abram rescued Lot out of precarious situations. On one occasion, he saved Lot from the eastern kings (Gen. 14:14–16). Another time, Abram rescued Lot from the destruction of Sodom and Gomorrah (Gen. 18:16–19:29). Even though God allowed Lot to be rescued, it did not mean that Lot would not suffer consequences for his actions. When leaving Sodom, Lot and his family were instructed not to look back, but his wife disobeyed. When she turned back, she became a pillar of salt (Gen. 19:26). Both Sodom and Gomorrah are believed to be buried under the Dead Sea. Ironically, salt is found in high quantity in the Dead Sea, making it easy to float on its waters. I cannot help but wonder if the high level of salt is left over from the destruction of Sodom and Gomorrah to remind all people of God's judgment.

Because he was growing old, Abram questioned God about the son that He had promised and God reassured him. "He (God) took him outside and said, 'Look up at the heavens and count the stars—if indeed you can count them.' So shall your offspring be'" (Gen. 15:5). Abram again showed his faith in God, and God blessed him (Gen. 15:6). Romans 4:20–21 expands on his faith. "Yet he did not waver through unbelief regarding the promise of God, but was strengthened in his faith and gave glory to God, being fully persuaded that God had power to do what he had promised." Through the example of Abram, we learn that God does not mind our asking questions of Him because when we ask, it gives Him the opportunity to reveal more of who He is. And in knowing God more, we can trust Him more.

Sarai knew of the promise of a son but believed she was too old. Instead of trusting in God, Sarai leaned on her own understanding. It was a custom of the day for the wife to give her maidservant to her husband to bear her a child if she was unable. Without looking to God for answers, Sarai gave her maidservant, Hagar, to Abram (Gen. 16:2). Hagar soon conceived. Sarai had acted out of what she thought was best, but all it brought was dissension in the family because Hagar, carrying Abram's child, despised Sarai. Sarai then cried out to Abram. I am sure that Abram was grieved but responded by telling her, "Your servant is in your hands. Do with her whatever you think best" (Gen. 16:6). The Bible says that Sarai was so cruel to her that Hagar fled. But the angel of the LORD came to Hagar with compassion and told her, "You are now with child and you will have a son. You shall name him Ishmael, for the LORD has heard your misery" (Gen. 16:11). The Bible says that after meeting the angel, Hagar returned to Abram and bore him Ishmael (Gen. 16:15).

Regardless of Sarai's lack of faith, God continued His covenant with Abram. As time went by, God revealed more of His promise. "When Abram was ninety-nine years old, the LORD appeared to him and said, 'I am God Almighty; walk before me and be blameless. I will confirm my covenant between me and you and will greatly increase your numbers'" (Gen. 17:1–2). And with this, God changed his name to Abraham because God made him a "father of many nations" (Gen. 17:5). Abraham humbled himself and worshiped God (Gen. 17:3). Then God revealed his covenant with Abraham as an everlasting covenant.

> God also said to Abraham, "As for Sarai your wife, you are no longer to call her Sarai; her name will be Sarah. I will bless her and will surely give you a son by her. I will bless her so that she will be the mother of nations; kings of peoples will come from her."
>
> Abraham fell facedown; he laughed and said to himself, "Will a son be born to a man a hundred years old? Will Sarah bear a child at the age of ninety?" And Abraham said to God, "If only Ishmael might live under your blessing!"
>
> Then God said, "Yes, but your wife Sarah will bear you a son, and you will call him Isaac. I will establish my covenant with him as an everlasting covenant for his descendants after him" (Gen. 17:15–19).

This promise from God was not dependent on Abraham or Sarah's actions but on God's actions. God wants us to understand that He has plans, and we can choose like Abram to be a part of them or we can choose to go our own way like Lot. No matter what we choose, His plans will stand firm with or without us (Ps. 33:11).

B. Isaac—the Son of Promise

Genesis 21 begins the story of the promised son, Isaac. The birth of Isaac is recorded in verses 1–5. When Isaac was eight days old, Abraham circumcised him as God had commanded (Gen. 21:4) God instituted circumcision as a sign of the covenant between Abraham and God (Gen. 17:9–10). Circumcision was a physical reminder to the family of Abraham that they were God's chosen people.

Abraham and Sarah loved Isaac. They anxiously anticipated the great things God would do through him. With God's promise given to Isaac, they knew he would be part of an extraordinary plan laid out by God Himself. But when Isaac was probably a young adult, the love Abraham had for God and Isaac was put to the test. God asked Abraham to trust Him with his son's very life when God commanded Abraham to sacrifice Isaac on an altar. "Take your son, your only son, Isaac, whom you love, and go to the region of Moriah. Sacrifice him there as a burnt offering on one of the mountains I will tell you about" (Gen. 22:2). Abraham never wavered in his trust and belief that this must be part of God's extraordinary plan for his son, Isaac. Hebrews 11:19 informs us, "Abraham reasoned that God could raise the dead, and figuratively speaking, he did receive Isaac back from death." Remember, at this time in history, no one had been raised from the dead. Still, Abraham trusted God. God was faithful to Abraham, for in the final moments, God supplied a ram as a sacrifice in the place of Isaac (Gen. 22:13). Because Abraham obeyed God, God promised him that through his offspring all nations would be blessed (Gen. 22:18).

Genesis 24 tells the love story of Abraham's servant finding Rebekah for Isaac. When you read about their meeting, the emotions can be felt through Scripture. Isaac was out in the field and saw the caravan of camels approaching, indicating the return of the servant with Isaac's bride. At the same moment, Rebekah, his betrothed, looked up from her seat in the caravan and saw Isaac standing in the field. She inquired who the man was, and when she was told, "she took her veil and covered herself" (Gen. 24:65). She was preparing to meet her husband. Even though they were strangers, there was great anticipation and intrigue. God loves a good love story. After they had been introduced, Isaac married her in the tent of his mother. The Bible says, "So she (Rebekah) became his wife, and he loved her; and Isaac was comforted after his mother's death" (Gen. 24:67). These words reveal a tenderness they immediately had for each other.

Sometime later after Sarah died, Abraham took another wife, Keturah (Gen. 25:1). Keturah bore him many children. He was generous with his children from Keturah, but Isaac was protected as heir. Everything went to Isaac because he was the son of promise (Gen. 25:5).

In Genesis, 26, the Abrahamic Covenant was confirmed to Isaac.

> *Now there was a famine in the land—besides the earlier famine of Abraham's time—and Isaac went to Abimelech king of the Philistines in Gerar. The LORD appeared to Isaac and said, "Do not go down to Egypt; live in the land where I tell you to live. Stay in this land for a while, and I will be with you and will bless you. For to you and your descendants I will give all these lands and will confirm the oath I swore to your father Abraham. I will make your descendants as numerous as the stars in the sky and will give them all these lands, and through your offspring all nations on earth will be blessed, because Abraham obeyed me and kept my requirements, my commands, my decrees and my laws." So Isaac stayed in Gerar* (Gen. 26:1–6).

Isaac obeyed God like his father, Abraham, and because of his obedience, all nations of the world were blessed through him. But, like his father, he was human as you or I.

Like his father, Isaac found himself being deceptive when he felt his life was in danger. When Isaac and his family had to travel to Gerar, the land of the Philistines, due to a famine, Isaac feared that Rebekah would be taken as the king's wife because she was very beautiful. The king's men asked him if Rebekah was his wife. Just like his father before him, instead of trusting God to take care of him, he lied and said that Rebekah was his sister (Gen. 26:7). When King Abimelech discovered the truth, he responded by rebuking Isaac for his deception just as Pharaoh had rebuked Abraham. Note that this happened right after God had confirmed His covenant with Isaac. Times of blessings are often followed by trials. We must be careful to not repeat the sins of our parents. Just as obedience is far reaching, so is sin.

C. Jacob and His Twelve Sons

Isaac fathered twins, Esau and Jacob (Gen. 25:24–26). The Bible tells of the struggle between the two in Rebekah's womb. At the birth, Esau was born first, but Jacob followed close behind holding the heel of Esau. Because Esau was the firstborn, by Hebrew tradition, he was to receive the birthright and blessing, but he did not honor his birthright. Instead, Esau treated his birthright lightly by selling it to Jacob for a bowl of stew (Gen. 25:27–34). God honored Esau's action by allowing Jacob to receive the blessing. But Jacob did not trust Esau to follow through with his commitment nor did he trust God to protect his newly bought inheritance. So with the help of his mother, Jacob deceived his father, Isaac, and was given the blessing of the oldest son (Gen. 27:1–33). This was accomplished by Jacob wearing the garments of Esau and going before his blind father claiming to be Esau. The Bible says Jacob then feared for his life because Esau resented him for stealing the blessing (Gen. 27:41). Rebekah recognized Jacob was in trouble and protected him by appealing to Isaac claiming that if Jacob married a woman of Canaan, she would be distraught (Gen. 27:46). This convenient urging from his mother allowed Jacob to escape the wrath of Esau and flee to Haran, also known as Padam Aram (Gen. 28:5). Jacob's deception caused years of turmoil for himself. He struggled with who he was and struggled with accepting the responsibility of the covenant between God and his family. Still, God pursued Jacob because He knew his heart.

On the way to Haran, God spoke to Jacob at Bethel. Here, God confirmed His covenant with Jacob. When he stopped for the night, Jacob laid down and used a stone as a pillow for his head. He had a dream where he saw a stairway that stretched from the earth to the heavens. On it, angels of God were traveling back and forth from heaven to earth (Gen. 28:12). In his dream, God spoke to him.

> *"I am the LORD, the God of your father Abraham and the God of Isaac. I will give you and your descendants the land on which you are lying. Your descendants will be like the dust of the earth, and you will spread out to the west and to the east, to the north and to the south. All peoples on earth will be blessed through you and your offspring. I am with you and will watch over you wherever you go, and I will bring you back to this land. I will not leave you until I have done what I have promised you"* (Gen. 28:13–15).

Early the next morning, Jacob took the stone on which he had rested his head and fashioned it into an altar to the Lord. "Then Jacob made a vow, saying, 'If God will be with me and will watch over me on this journey I am taking and will give me food to eat and clothes to wear so that I return safely to my father's house, then the LORD will be my God and this stone that I have set up as a pillar will be God's house, and of all that you give me I will give you a tenth'" (Gen. 28:20–22). Notice that Jacob put stipulations on God: "If God will… give me food to eat and clothes to wear….. then…" But God continued to be patient with Jacob. It reminds us that even when we struggle to trust God, He remains faithful to us.

On the outskirts of Haran, Jacob found some shepherds by a well. He asked them if they knew Laban. They pointed out his daughter Rachel coming to the well with her sheep. The Bible says that while they were talking, Jacob removed the stone from the well and gave his uncle's sheep some water (Gen. 29:10). With a kiss, he introduced himself to Rachel as the son of Rebekah, her father's sister (Gen. 29:11–12). The Bible says that Rachel immediately left to tell her father about Jacob (Gen. 29:12). Laban then came and brought Jacob back to his home, and Jacob stayed with Laban and worked his land.

After working the fields for only a month, Jacob fell in love with Rachel. An agreement was made that Jacob would work for Laban seven years for Rachel's hand (Gen. 29:18). But because the oldest daughter Leah was not married by the completion of those years, Laban tricked Jacob into marrying Leah. Because Jacob loved Rachel, he agreed to work another seven years for Rachel. Laban allowed Jacob to marry Rachel after the week celebration of his marriage to Leah. Then Jacob worked the remaining years for the price of his Rachel. This Jacob did willingly (Gen 28:27–28).

During the years that Jacob worked for Laban, his family grew, his wealth grew, and God multiplied his cattle (Gen. 30:43). These blessings caused grumblings within the family of Laban. Laban's sons accused Jacob of getting wealthy by taking what belonged to their father (Gen. 31:1–2). "Then the LORD said to Jacob, 'Go back to the land of your fathers and to your relatives, and I will be with you'" (Gen. 31:3). Jacob immediately packed his family and left without saying goodbye to Laban. Three days after Jacob's family fled, Laban heard of their departure. He pursued Jacob (Gen. 31:23). On his way, God came to Laban and cautioned him about speaking to Jacob. When Laban overtook Jacob at Gilead, they made a covenant to be at peace (Gen. 31:51–54). Laban returned home (Gen. 31:55), and Jacob continued his journey back to the land of his father (Gen. 32:1).

While on his journey home, Jacob came face to face with not only God but with who he was and God's promise to him. In Genesis 32, as he was preparing to meet Esau, he sent his family along with the entire caravan ahead of him across the ford of the Jabbok. There he was left alone on the shore by a stream. An angel of the Lord appeared and struggled with Jacob throughout the night. In the morning, the man asked Jacob to let go of him. "But Jacob replied, 'I will not let you go unless you bless me.' The man asked him, 'What is your name?' 'Jacob,' he answered" (Gen. 32:26–27). This was a defining moment. In those early morning hours, Jacob finally came to terms with who he was and accepted God's plan for his life. At that moment, God changed Jacob's name to seal the covenant and to remind him of who he was. "Then the man said, 'Your name will no longer be Jacob, but Israel, because you have struggled with God and with men and have overcome'" (Gen. 32:28). The Bible says, "Jacob called the place Peniel, saying, 'It is because I saw God face to face, and yet my life was spared.'" This experience humbled Jacob.

In the next chapter of Genesis, Jacob humbles himself before Esau. His posture had changed because he had been changed. And from this meeting, the two brothers separate in peace (Gen. 33:15–16). When we allow God to work in our hearts, He works in our lives and blesses us.

Unfortunately, Jacob's change in name and posture does not make him or his family immune to sin. In Genesis 34, the sin of revenge grows in the hearts of Jacob's sons when their sister Dinah is raped by a Canaanite. Without consulting God or Jacob, Simeon, and Levi devised a plan to attack and kill all the men of the city (Gen. 34:25). After they succeeded in their plan, Jacob realized what had happened and feared for his family's life. So in chapter 35, we read that God sent Jacob back to Bethel to protect them. Jacob also recognized that he needed to worship and purify the family just as Abraham, his grandfather, had done so many times at Bethel. When sin enters into our life, we need to pull back and spend time with God in renewing our souls to Him. God was with Jacob. So God put a fear in the people of the land where Jacob's family would be protected. God reminded Jacob of His blessing to him and again told him that he would no longer be called Jacob, but Israel (Gen. 35:10). God is faithful even when we are not.

Shortly after God reconfirmed His covenant with Jacob, the Bible tells that Rachel died giving birth to Benjamin (Gen. 35:17–18). It is not until later that the Bible reveals that Jacob was devastated by her death (Gen. 48:7). Benjamin becomes the last of the twelve sons of Jacob: Reuben, Simeon, Levi, Judah, Zebulun, Issachar, Dan, Gad, Asher, Naphtali, Joseph, and Benjamin (Gen. 35:23–26). Later, from these sons, comes the twelve tribes of Israel.

D. Joseph–The Deliverer

Many will find this section of history familiar. It is a well-known and a beloved Bible story—the story of Joseph and the coat of many colors. Why was he given such a colorful coat in a time when color was expensive and a rarity? The answer is favoritism. The Bible says, "Now Israel loved Joseph more than any of his other sons, because he had been born to him in his old age; and he made a richly ornamented robe for him" (Gen. 37:3). His brothers recognized the favoritism and were jealous of Joseph. He not only wore his prized coat for all to see, but he also shared with his brothers dreams that appeared to reveal them bowing down to him. This further infuriated his brothers. Even Scripture tells that on one occasion, Jacob, his father, rebuked him for such dreams (Gen. 37:10). Still, Joseph was young and proud of the status and position he had been given.

One day Jacob told Joseph to go to the Valley of Hebron to check on his brothers and their flocks (Gen. 37:14). He departed wearing his coat in the blazing hot sun. When he finally arrived, his brothers saw him from a distance and were filled with jealousy. "Here comes that dreamer!" (Gen. 37:19). The brothers could no longer tolerate the favored son's foolish pride and initially plotted to kill him until they were persuaded by their brother Judah to instead sell him to a caravan of Ishmaelites (Gen. 37:25–27). They told their father that Joseph had been killed by wild animals and produced his coat that they had covered with goat's blood as evidence (Gen. 37:31). The Bible says that Jacob was inconsolable in his grief (Gen. 37:35). But what man planned for evil, God used for good.

The Ishmaelites brought Joseph to Egypt, where the captain of the guard to Pharaoh bought him to work as a slave in his home (Gen. 39:1). "The LORD was with Joseph and he prospered..." (Gen. 39:2). Many things happened to Joseph, but God was always with him. Being sold into slavery, falsely accused of a crime he did not commit, and then thrown into jail, Joseph lost his younger cocky self. He became humbled before God. Not until we are humbled can we be blessed in helping God with His work.

While in jail, Joseph was called by Pharaoh to come before his presence and interpret two dreams (Gen. 41:14–36). These dreams warned of a famine that would affect the land in the years to come. Not only did God give Joseph the ability to interpret the dreams, but God also gave him a plan to save Egypt from the impending famine. Joseph shared this plan with Pharaoh and was placed second in command over all of Egypt (Gen. 41:39–43).

When the famine struck, it not only affected Egypt but all the surrounding areas. Joseph had directed the people to prepare for the famine, so Egypt was prepared. But like others outside of Egypt, Joseph's father and brothers suffered. When the family had exhausted their supply of food, Jacob sent ten of his sons to Egypt for needed staples. Little did the brothers know that when they stood before the governor of Egypt asking for food, they were standing face to face with the brother, whom they had sold into slavery (Gen. 42:6). Joseph recognized them immediately but chose to keep his identity a secret until he could test them to see if they had changed. After being reassured that their hearts had changed, he could hide his identity no longer. "I am Joseph!" (Gen. 45:3). The brothers were afraid at first. Of course, who would not be? But Joseph reassured them, "God sent me ahead of you to preserve for you a remnant on earth and to save your lives by a great deliverance" (Gen. 45:7). Joseph recognized the hand of God preserving the promise to Abraham.

With excitement beyond words, Jacob was finally brought by his sons to Joseph. On his way, God encouraged Jacob. "I am God, the God of your father. Do not be afraid to go down to Egypt, for I will make you into a great nation there. I will go down to Egypt with you, and I will surely bring you back again. And Joseph's own hand will close your eyes" (Gen. 46:3–4). Upon the family's arrival in Egypt, Jacob and his family settled in the land of Goshen. Jacob lived there another seventeen years before he died (Gen. 47:28). After his father's death, Joseph took him back to Canaan to be buried where Abraham and Sarah were buried just like he had promised (Gen. 50:12–14).

But before Jacob died, we find in Genesis 48–49, he gave a blessing to each of his sons. Joseph is the only son not directly blessed. Instead, Jacob blessed his sons, Ephraim and Manasseh. This was a double blessing to Joseph through his children. Is there no greater blessing to a parent than when God blesses their children? Manasseh was the oldest, but Jacob puts Ephraim ahead of Manasseh, which is similar to what occurred between Jacob and Esau (Gen. 48:20). Later, the Israelites, the descendants of Abraham, are many times referred to as Ephraimites. When the land of Canaan is divided among the tribes, the city of Shiloh in Ephraim was blessed with housing the holy tabernacle during the period of the Judges.

After Jacob's death, Joseph made the brothers swear that when God brought them back to Canaan, they would carry his bones back to Canaan (Gen. 50:24–25). He knew Egypt was not his home.

Several hundred years later, when Moses led the Israelites out of Egypt, Joseph's descendants remembered the vow made by Joseph's brothers to Joseph and carried the bones of Joseph back to the land of promise (Exod. 13:19). The Bible says upon entering the Promised Land, his bones were buried in Shechem, which was close to where he had been sold by his brothers into slavery (Gen. 37:14–17; Josh. 24:32). Joseph obeyed God and was able to be used instrumentally in saving the future Israelites from extinction. And because of his faithfulness, God allowed him to be brought home and buried in the place of his youth, the Promised Land.

E. Israel in Egypt

When Jacob and his family moved to Egypt, there were seventy members (Deut. 10:22). Over the next 430 years (Exod. 12:40), they grew into a large nation that was as numerous as the stars in the sky (Deut. 1:10). The Bible says, "The Israelites were fruitful and multiplied greatly and became exceedingly numerous, so that the land was filled with them" (Exod. 1:7). As their numbers grew, the Egyptians became fearful and enslaved them because they feared that the Israelites would eventually rebel and leave Egypt (Exod. 1:8–10). Their fear was not unfounded. Although there was no rebellion, divine intervention was at work because God had promised the land of Canaan to Abraham and his descendants (Gen. 35:12). When God decided it was time, He put His plan into action.

III. The Exodus and the Years of Wandering

Exodus, Numbers, and Deuteronomy tell the story of God bringing His people out of bondage in Egypt and into the land of Canaan. Remember, this was the same land where Jacob lived with his family until Joseph called them to come live in Egypt because of the famine.

The Connection of Christ from Garden to Cross

During the time of Abraham, Isaac, and Jacob, the land was only promised (Gen. 48:3–4). It was not theirs to claim. When God delivered His people out of Egypt, He was fulfilling His promise by giving the descendants of the three patriarchs (Abraham, Isaac, and Jacob) the land for all generations. But before they entered the land, the Israelites had much to learn about trusting God. Their journey to the Promised Land was not a simple task. It took forty years of God teaching the Israelites who He is and how to trust in Him.

The story of the Exodus begins with the nation of Israel enslaved by the Egyptians. In Chapter 2 of Exodus, we read that the Israelites were groaning and crying out in their bondage (Gen. 2:23). Interestingly, the Bible does not mention that they cried out to God, but the Bible says, "God heard their groaning and he remembered his covenant with Abraham, with Isaac and with Jacob. So God looked on the Israelites and was concerned about them" (Gen. 2:24–25). God did not rescue the Israelites because He was asked. He rescued them because He had compassion.

At the beginning of Exodus 2, we are introduced to the deliverer of the Israelites. We find the deliverer in a small, papyrus basket hidden within the reeds of the Nile River. Pharaoh had begun to kill all the Israelite baby boys because of his fear of their numbers increasing (Exod. 1:22). But this little boy was rescued by Pharaoh's daughter and named Moses (Exod. 2:5–10). For the first forty years of his life (Acts 7:23), Moses lived in the palace until the day he found himself wanted for murder of an Egyptian slave master (Exod. 2:11–15). He then fled to the land of Midian, where he lived the next forty years of his life in the desert as a shepherd (Acts 7:30). It was there that he took Zipporah, a shepherdess, as his wife (Exod. 2:21). Moses's life is a great example that shows sometimes it takes time for God to prepare a person to do His work. Moses lived forty years in the palace, learning and understanding the ways of Egyptian royalty and then forty years in the desert learning to live and prosper off the land. What perfect training ground for the man who would go before Pharaoh and lead the Israelites through the wilderness. We might not understand where we are and what God is doing in our lives, but if we are trusting in Him, we can be assured that He is preparing us for His work.

One day while living in the land of Midian (Acts 7:29–30), Moses was out keeping his flock. It was here that God called him through a burning bush that was not being consumed by the fire (Exod. 3:1–2).

> *God called to him from within the bush, "Moses! Moses!"*
>
> *And Moses said, "Here I am."*
>
> *"Do not come any closer," God said. "Take off your sandals, for the place where you are standing is holy ground." Then he said, "I am the God of your father, the God of Abraham, the God of Isaac and the God of Jacob." At this, Moses hid his face, because he was afraid to look at God.*
>
> *The LORD said, "I have indeed seen the misery of my people in Egypt. I have heard them crying out because of their slave drivers, and I am concerned about their suffering. So I have come down to rescue them from the hand of the Egyptians and to bring them up out of that land into a good and spacious land, a land flowing with milk and honey—the home of the Canaanites, Hittites, Amorites, Perizzites, Hivites and Jebusites. And now the cry of the Israelites has reached me, and I have seen the way the Egyptians are oppressing them. So now, go. I am sending you to Pharaoh to bring my people the Israelites out of Egypt"* (Exod. 3:4–10).

Every time I read this account, I marvel that Moses did not run away from those flames screaming wildly. If I saw a burning bush that called out my name, I am pretty sure I would run as fast as I could to put some distance between it and me. But God knew Moses. It is obvious that he had already prepared his heart for this calling because immediately Moses answered without hesitation, "Here I am" (Exod. 3:4). The time in Midian gave him many years to think about who he was and *whom* he belonged to. Still, Moses questioned God's choice in him (Exod. 3:11) because he lacked confidence in himself. Moses soon learned that anyone God calls is sufficient to do His work because God enables him.

As he was instructed, Moses returned to Egypt with Aaron (Exod. 4:29–31), but God did not immediately allow His people to leave their captivity. He first dealt with the Egyptians. Starting in chapter 7 of Exodus, we see the beginning of the ten plagues God unleashed on Egypt because of the hardening of Pharaoh's heart. Each plague targeted one of their gods or goddesses. These gods and goddesses were symbols of creation. Instead of worshiping the One True God, the Egyptians were worshiping God's creation. Through the plagues, God was showing the Egyptians that He was the Creator, the One True God of all creation, the God of all gods. After the plague of death that took his first born son and all the first born males of Egypt, Pharaoh finally relented and allowed the Israelites to leave Egypt (Exod. 12:29–30). This final plague would from that day forward be celebrated by the Israelites as the Feast of Passover in remembrance of God's death angel passing over the Israelites' homes (Exod. 13:3–16), sparing their firstborn because of His mercy (Exod. 12:23). Pharaoh had had enough. He commanded Moses to take the people and go (Exod. 12:31). Of course, later he had a change of heart and went after the Israelites, but by then it was too late.

Moses led the children of Israel out of Egypt to the Red Sea, where God parted the waters, allowing the Israelites to cross over out of the land of bondage (Exod. 14:21–22). During their travels, God gave them everything they needed: a cloud to guide them by day and a pillar of fire to guide them by night (Exod. 13:21–22), manna for food (Exod. 16:4–5), and clothes that did not wear out and feet that never swelled on their travels (Deut. 8:4). God even had them build a tabernacle (Exod. 25:8) where He met with Moses "above the cover between the two cherubim that are over the ark of the Testimony" (Exod. 25:22). Exodus records the journey of the Israelites as far as their travel to Mount Sinai, where they built the tabernacle and the Shekinah Glory of God descended upon it (Exod. 40:34–35). It is here that God gave the Israelites the Law, which included the Ten Commandments (Exod. 20:1–17).

In the beginning chapters of Numbers, God led the people from Mount Sinai to the land of promise. Chapter 13 records the arrival of the Israelites at the edge of the Promised Land. God chose one leader from each tribe to enter and explore the land (Num. 13:1–2). Moses did as God instructed, but after going into the land, not all the spies trusted God would give them the land. Instead, ten of the twelve spies recommended that the Israelites not go in for fear that the giants of the land would overtake them (Num. 13:27–29, 31). But the other two spies, Joshua and Caleb, gave a different report. "We should go up and take possession of the land, for we can certainly do it" (Num. 13:30). But the Israelites chose to grumble against Moses and Aaron because they believed the region was unattainable and that God had led them to a land they had no hope of conquering (Num. 14:1–4). They did not listen to the promise of the Lord nor did they listen to the spies that trusted in God. Instead, the people chose to disobey God and not enter. For their disobedience, God said, "For forty years—one year for each of the forty days you explored the land—you will suffer for your sins and know what it is like to have me against you." (Num. 14:34). During the years of wandering, every person twenty years and older, except for Joshua and Caleb, died in the wilderness (Num. 14:29–30). The lesson to learn is that when we choose not to obey God, He will raise up others to do His work. The adults that came out of Egypt had the opportunity to enter the land of promise and be blessed, but they chose to disobey. Because of this, their offspring inherited their blessing.

Moses and Aaron were also not allowed to enter the land of promise because at Meribah Kadesh in the wilderness, they did not obey God. "The LORD said to Moses and Aaron, 'Because you did not trust in me enough to honor me as holy in the sight of the Israelites, you will not bring this community into the land I give them'" (Num. 20:12). This might seem harsh, but God is a just God. When God enables us to do His work, He demands that we give Him the glory. But God is also a merciful God. When it was time for the Israelites to go into the land, God brought Moses to the top of Mount Nebo and showed him the region promised to Abraham, Isaac, and Jacob (Deut. 34:1–4). The Bible says, "There the LORD showed him the whole land" (Deut. 34:1). Can you imagine this moment between God and Moses? No matter what was discussed, I have no doubt God reassured Moses that He would always be with His people. Promises of God are far-reaching, and although day to day we might not always understand, God is always with us (Heb. 13:5) and He always keeps His promises (Deut. 7:9).

IV. The Conquest of Canaan

The book of Joshua begins where the book of Deuteronomy ends. Determined to follow God's instruction after forty years of wandering in the desert, the nation of Israel stood on the east side of the Jordan River, but this time ready to claim the land of promise. God chose Joshua to lead His people into the Promised Land. Deuteronomy 34:9 shares the passing of the leadership rod: "Now Joshua son of Nun was filled with the spirit of wisdom because Moses had laid his hands on him. So the Israelites listened to him and did what the LORD had commanded Moses."

Before entering the land, Joshua reminded the Reubenites, the Gadites, and the half-tribe of Mannasseh, whom were granted the land east of the Jordan that their able-bodied men were to enter Canaan with the rest of the Israelites to help take possession. Then they could return to their land to possess it (Josh. 1:12–15). These two and a half tribes recognized their responsibility and promised to obey Joshua's every word (Josh. 1:16–18). With this, the people were prepared to enter the land.

Then Joshua sent two spies to investigate the land, "especially Jericho" (Josh. 2:1). When they came to Jericho, a prostitute named Rahab hid them in her home. There had been much discussion throughout Canaan concerning how the God of the Israelites had dried up the Red Sea for them to cross and had given them many victories against their enemies in the desert. Rahab believed that God had already given the Israelites the land of Canaan; she feared for her life and her family's life. Recognizing the power of God, she made the spies swear to her that she and her family would be spared. In Joshua 2:17–18, we read the sign of her salvation. "The men said to her, 'This oath you made us swear will not be binding on us unless, when we enter the land, you have tied this scarlet cord in the window through which you let us down, and unless you have brought your father and mother and your brothers and all your family into your house.'" When the two spies returned, they said to Joshua, "The LORD has surely given the whole land into our hands; all the people are melting in fear because of us" (Josh. 2:24). Notice that even with impending destruction, God was willing to hear the cry of Rahab, who recognized Him as the One True God. This shows that God wants all people to know Him, and He is ready to listen when people call on His name. Yes, the Israelites were God's chosen people, but they were chosen to show all the people of the world who He is so that all would know Him. Therefore, when Rahab cried out, God heard her cry and had compassion.

An interesting fact to note is that Rahab was the great-great-grandmother of King David (Matt. 1:5–6). God blessed Rahab's faith. From her line came the Savior of the world! This shows us that no matter who we are or where we come from, if we turn to God, He will bless us and use us in His divine work.

After the spies returned, the Israelites were ready to enter the land. I can almost feel the excitement as they leaned forward at the ready—anxious to enter at God's command. With the blessings of the Almighty God, Joshua led Israel dry-shod over the Jordan River into the Promised Land (Josh. 3:4–17). As God commanded, Joshua had twelve stones piled on each other on the west side of the Jordan as a memorial to remind the people and their descendants of this day (Josh. 4:8–9). What a day this must have been! The land that was promised to Abraham years ago was now laid out before his descendants, ready to be taken.

Now that they were going in to claim the land, they needed to be reminded to *whom* they belonged. During the years of wandering, the practice of circumcision had not taken place. Since all the people twenty years of age and older had died in the desert, no male was circumcised except Caleb and Joshua, whom the Lord spared (Josh. 5:4–5). Therefore, circumcision was necessary before the Israelites could begin their campaign to conquer the land. Remember, God initiated circumcision to remind the people of His covenant with them (Gen. 17:12–14).

When the men were healed, the people celebrated the Feast of the Passover (Josh. 5:10). During this day of celebration, the Israelites ate from the produce of the land. The next day, the manna from heaven stopped (Josh. 5:12). God had provided for them in the desert. From this point on, God would provide for them with the harvest from their claimed land.

The siege of the land began with the battle of Jericho (Josh. 6). For six days, God commanded Joshua to have the people march around Jericho once daily with the seven priests blowing their trumpets in the lead followed by the Ark of the Covenant. On the seventh day, they marched around the city seven times again with the trumpets sounding. But, after the seventh round when the people heard the priest blow a long blast, Joshua commanded the people to shout! When the people gave a loud shout, the walls of Jericho fell down, and the Israelites charged into the city and overtook it. Here all the silver and gold taken from the city went into the Lord's treasury as God had commanded. The only inhabitants that were spared from the complete destruction were Rahab and her family, who were protected within the walls of her home because she had hidden the spies. The Bible says that she went to live among the Israelites the remainder of her years (Jos. 6:25).

From Jericho, the Israelites marched to Ai. The first attempt at taking the city failed (Josh. 7:4–5). Joshua then questioned God and discovered Achan's sin. He had kept some of the plunder from Jericho (Josh. 7:20–21). After Achan's sin was dealt with, Joshua, with God's blessing, took the city by ambushing the soldiers outside the walls. This time God allowed success and the Israelites were allowed to keep the plunder (Josh. 8:1–2, 27). From there, the Israelite army marched south. Then they went north invading more of the land. By a series of decisive campaigns, much of the inhabitants of Canaan were defeated.

In Chapter 10 of Joshua is an interesting story of how the sun stood still. The city of Gibeon had made a treaty of peace with the nation of Israel. This was no ordinary city. It was important and compared to royalty. The Amorites heard about the alliance between the Israelites and the Gibeonites and determined it would be a strategic move against the Israelites to capture the city. Upon hearing of their plan, the Gibeonites sent word to Joshua for assistance. Joshua asked the Lord for guidance, and God reassured him that the battle was theirs. Joshua then marched his army to Gibeon and fought the Amorites bravely. So fierce was the battle that the Amorites fled. As they fled, the Bible says that the Lord hurled huge hailstones from the sky that brought down more soldiers than the swords of the Israelites had killed (Gen. 10:11). When the Amorites were defeated, Joshua, in the presence of the Israelites, asked the Lord to have the sun and moon stand still. The Bible says, "So the sun stood still, and the moon stopped, till the nation avenged itself on its enemies… The sun stopped in the middle of the sky and delayed going down about a full day. There has never been a day like it before or since, a day when the LORD listened to a man. Surely the LORD was fighting for Israel!" (Josh. 10:13–14). Through this miracle, all saw God's power and might. Joshua believed God, and God blessed Him by allowing him and all the people to see His marvelous works!

When Joshua was old, God told him there was still land that needed to be conquered in Canaan (Josh. 13:1). By the Lord's instruction, Joshua divided the land among the tribes of Israel and commanded them to carry forward the conquest until their enemies were subdued and they were in full possession of their land. The only tribe that would not have land allocated to them was the tribe of Levi, who would be provided for by the other tribes. These allocations are found in Joshua 13–19.

As part of the division of the land, Joshua established a central place for worship, chose forty-eight cities for the Levites, and designated six cities of refuge. The central place chosen for all of Israel to worship was Shiloh in the land of Ephraim (Josh. 18:1). To offer sacrifice, it was necessary for the Israelites to travel to Shiloh, but in their individual cities, they could worship the Lord with the assistance of the Levites. This is why the Levites were not given an inheritance of land. Their inheritance was to serve as priests among the tribes and to be provided for by the people. They were also given pastureland for their livestock. The cities of refuge were designated to be safe havens. These were designated places for a person who kills another unintentionally. Here they would be safe until they went before an assembly for trial (Josh. 20:1–3). This was necessary for the person to be protected from retribution.

One of the final commands Joshua gave was for the two and a half tribes to return to the eastern side of the Jordan and subdue their lands. He also reminded them to follow the Lord in all ways. Then Joshua blessed them and sent them on their way (Josh. 22:1–6).

Just before Joshua's death, he appealed to the people to be faithful to God (Josh. 24:14). There was no doubt of Joshua's heart. He loved his God, and He loved his people. He encouraged the Israelites to choose to obey God. As a true leader, Joshua led by example with this commitment: "But as for me and my household, we will serve the LORD" (Josh. 24:15). Joshua's life showed his commitment to the Lord, and the Lord showed His commitment to Joshua by being with Joshua all the days of his life. The people of Israel promised that day to serve God and obey him (Josh. 24:24). But the nation did not always keep its promise. Because of this, the nation struggled in its land and in its independence. But God remained faithful to His people.

V. The Judges

The time period of the Judges is recorded in the books of Judges and Ruth. After the glorious days of Moses and Joshua came the mournful days of the Judges. These years were filled with failure and defeat that was a direct result of the Israelites' disobedience to God. God had given them everything they needed: a land to claim as their own, a law to live by, and a central place of worship located in Shiloh to sacrifice to Him. But, unlike times past, God did not raise up an earthly leader. Instead, God directly ruled over Israel. Israel was to obey God's laws, and God promised to protect and provide for His people.

As long as Joshua lived, the Israelites were faithful to God (Josh. 24:31). But after Joshua's death, the Israelites found themselves in a continuous cycle that began with the Israelites slowly turning from God and worshiping other gods, like Baal and the Ashtoreth idols. This disobedience broke the Israelites' covenant with God, which hindered their relationship with Him. God would then remove His hand of protection, which would allow the neighboring peoples to conquer them. Then the Israelites would cry out to God to end their suffering. God would, in turn, hear their cries and raise up a judge to save them. "Whenever the LORD raised up a judge for them, he was with the judge and saved them out of the hands of their enemies as long as the judge lived; for the LORD had compassion on them as they groaned under those who oppressed and afflicted them" (Judg. 2:18). There were twelve judges God raised up during these years. A judge was to convict the Israelites of their sin. Once the people had returned to God, the judge acted as a military leader to deliver them from their oppressors. Once the people had been delivered, the judge was responsible for administering justice and keeping the people focused on God. The Bible goes on to say that when the judge died, the people would return to their wicked ways and again worship other gods. This would cause the cycle to begin all over again (Judg. 2:11–23). The dominate theme in the book of Judges is summed up in these words: "In those days Israel had no king; everyone did as he saw fit" (Josh. 17:6; 18:1; 19:1; 21:25). Because of their disobedience, God did not permit the Israelites to drive out all the people of the land. Instead, He allowed the gods of the land to become a snare to the people of Israel (Judg. 2:3).

Starting in Chapter 13 of Judges, a familiar story from Sunday school comes to life as we read about Samson, one of the judges of Israel. Like many other people chosen by God to do His work, Samson did not always follow the will of God. Desperate to know the secret of his strength, the leaders of the Philistines came to Delilah, whom Samson had fallen in love with, and bribed her with 1100 shekels of silver from each Philistine ruler to convince Samson to tell her the secret of his strength (Judg. 16:5). What God had demanded to be kept secret, Samson was soon persuaded by Delilah to reveal. His God-given strength was in the length of his hair (Judg. 16:17). This led to his demise. In death, Samson turned back to God for strength to defeat the Philistines. As he was tied to the temple pillars of Dagon, Samson pushed the pillars down on the Philistines (Judg. 16:28–30). The Bible says, "…he killed many more when he died than while he lived" (Judg. 16:30). The story of Samson teaches us that God recognizes that we will fail. What is important to Him is how we choose to react to our failure.

The book of Ruth is a story that occurred during the time of the Judges. Again, we see God at work. The Bible records that a man and his family from Bethlehem traveled to Moab, where they lived to wait out a famine in Judah. While in Moab, the two sons married Moabite women, Ruth and Orpah. Later the father and the two sons died. His widow, Naomi, then heard that there was again food in Judah, so she decided to return home with her two daughter-in-laws. After they began their journey, Naomi became concerned for the two women's welfare, and she urged them to return to their families. Orpah chose to return to her family. "But Ruth replied, 'Don't urge me to leave you or to turn back from you. Where you go I will go, and where you stay I will stay. Your people will be my people and your God my God. Where you die I will die, and there I will be buried. May the Lord deal with me, be it ever so severely, if anything but death separates you and me'" (Ruth 1:16–17). When Naomi realized Ruth's determination, the two traveled on to Bethlehem. Because they were poor, Ruth had to glean from the fields to find food for Naomi and herself. This was very dangerous work for a woman, but God protected her. Boaz, the landowner, found favor in Ruth. The book of Ruth tells the beautiful love story of Ruth and Boaz. The importance of these individuals in history is that their great-grandchild was King David, who was a direct ancestor of Jesus (Matt. 1:6). Again, God protected the line of Jesus even in the dangerous grainfields of Canaan.

VI. The Kingdom of Israel

Samuel was a prophet and the final judge for Israel (1 Sam. 3:20–21; 7:15). The period of the Kingdom began when God commanded Samuel to anoint the first king of Israel (1 Sam. 8:21–22). The nation had rejected God as ruler and desired instead an earthly king like the other nations (1 Sam. 8:6–9). God heard the Israelites' request but gave warning. "This is what the king who will reign over you will do … When that day comes, you will cry out for relief from the king you have chosen, and the LORD will not answer you in that day" (1 Sam. 8:11–18). The *Scofield Study Bible: New International Version* notes: "The demand of Israel, as recorded in this chapter did not mean the end of the theocratic kingdom. Although it implied a rejection of God, the people's demand was granted only in part. They were given a king, but certainly not 'as all the other nations.' God is always sovereign over the nations in providential control but in this instance He reserved for Himself the right to choose the king by direct control, and the king was made personally responsible to God for his actions, thus clearly indicating an unbroken continuance of the LORD's particular sovereignty over the nation."[6] God honored the nation's desire, but God remained in control of His people and His plan.

A. Saul's Reign

In a private ceremony, Saul was anointed the first king of Israel by Samuel (1 Sam. 10:1). 1 Samuel 9:1–2 describes him as a man of great stature: "There was a Benjamite, a man of standing, whose name was Kish son of Abiel… He had a son named Saul, an impressive young man without equal among the Israelites—a head taller than any of the others." God chose Saul with the desires of the people in mind. The Bible records this when Samuel said to Saul, "And to whom is all the desire of Israel turned, if not to you and all your father's family?" (1 Sam. 9:20). This shows that man looks at the physical appearance to determine ability, but God looks at the heart when he chooses men to do His work (1 Sam. 16:7). When we get to the second king, we will see this difference.

In present day New Testament time, the Spirit of God enters a believer when a person accepts Christ as Savior (1 John 3:24). Once the Spirit enters, He does not leave (Heb. 13:5). This was not the case during Old Testament days. Before the cross, the Spirit of God entered an individual for a period of time to accomplish a task for God. There are only a few recorded instances of this occurring. One recorded occurrence was when God anointed Saul king over Israel; God's Spirit came upon him (1 Sam. 10:9–10). As long as Saul was obedient, the Spirit of God remained with him.

Saul began his reign obeying God, but there came a time when he turned from God's direction. Often he caved to pressure like the time he feared the Philistines' attack on the Israelites at Gilgal. Only the priests could sacrifice offerings on the altar, but Saul's fear compelled him to light the altars to ask God for favor in battle (1 Sam. 13:12). When Samuel the prophet arrived before the attack and rebuked Saul's choice, Saul defended his actions with excuses. Because of Saul's repeated disobedience, God removed the kingship from him and gave it to a man of God's choosing, "a man after His own heart" (1 Sam. 13:13–14). Samuel informed Saul, "The LORD has torn the kingdom of Israel from you today and has given it to one of your neighbors—to one better than you" (1 Sam. 15:28).

1 Samuel 16 introduces us to the second king of Israel, David. "So he (Jesse, David's father) sent and had him brought in. He was ruddy, with a fine appearance and handsome features. Then the LORD said, 'Rise and anoint him; he is the one'" (1 Sam. 16:12). After Samuel anointed David, immediately we read, "The Spirit of the LORD came upon David with power" (1 Sam. 16:13). The next verse informs us that "The Spirit of the Lord had departed from Saul" (1 Sam. 16:14). Because of Saul's pride, God could no longer use him. Are you not thankful that because we live after the cross as followers of Jesus Christ, the Spirit of God will never leave us (Heb. 13:5)? But oh, how I never want to become an unusable vessel for God!

David came to know Saul. His first encounter with him was when David was asked to play the harp when Saul was tormented by evil spirits. The Bible says, "Now the Spirit of the LORD had departed from Saul, and an evil spirit from the LORD tormented him" (1 Sam. 16:14). This might sound a bit confusing. You might ask yourself, "Why would God send an evil spirit into Saul?" But, the Bible does not say that God sent an evil spirit into Saul. The Bible says, "An evil spirit from the LORD tormented him" (1 Sam. 16:14). To understand this, let us look at the comparison between light and darkness. Science defines light, but darkness is defined as the absence of light. Likewise, the absence of God is evil. Just like light does not produce darkness, neither does God produce evil. Because Saul had known the Spirit of God by His indwelling, it makes sense that the absence of God would be tormenting. It is then understandable why David playing the harp soothed the spirit of Saul.

1 Samuel 17 is one of the most known stories of the Bible. It records the story of how David defeated Goliath with only a sling and one smooth stone. It was with this victory the people of Israel started seeing David as a man worthy of recognition. "As they danced, they sang: 'Saul has slain his thousands, and David his tens of thousands'" (1 Sam. 18:7). This angered Saul and jealousy was born in his heart (1 Sam. 18:8–9). He knew the Lord was with David in everything he did, which caused Saul not only to become fearful of David but also to be jealous of his position. Saul sent him away to command his troops, but David continued to prosper and all of Israel and Judah respected him (1 Sam. 18:12–16). For the remainder of his life, Saul pursued David, but because David had respect for God, he respected the first anointed king of Israel because God had anointed Saul. There were times that David could have harmed Saul but chose to honor God. It was not until the death of Saul at Mount Gilboa against the Philistines that David rested. But still, he and his men mourned Saul's death (2 Sam. 1:11–12).

B. David's Reign

After Saul's death, God told David to travel to Hebron in Judah (2 Sam. 2:1). The men of Judah met David in Hebron and anointed him king over Judah. It was seven years and six months later that he was anointed king over all of Israel. He ruled for an additional thirty-three years. David reigned a total of forty years (2 Sam. 5:4–5).

After becoming king of Israel, David and his men marched to Jerusalem and overpowered the city. There, David settled in Jerusalem and named it the City of David (2 Sam. 5:6–9). The Bible says that David became more powerful because God was with him (2 Sam. 5:10).

Because of David's love for the Lord, he desired to build a temple where the Lord God might have a dwelling place among the Israelites (2 Sam. 7:1–2). Instead, God chose to honor David's request through his offspring. God revealed to Nathan, a prophet, an eternal covenant between God and David.

> *Go and tell my servant David, "This is what the LORD says: Are you the one to build me a house to dwell in? I have not dwelt in a house from the day I brought the Israelites up out of Egypt to this day. I have been moving from place to place with a tent as my dwelling… When your days are over and you rest with your fathers, I will raise up your offspring to succeed you, who will come from your own body, and I will establish his kingdom. He is the one who will build a house for my Name, and I will establish the throne of his kingdom forever. I will be his father, and he will be my son… Your house and your kingdom will endure forever before me; your throne will be established forever"* (2 Sam. 7:5–16).

David was humbled by God's promise. "Who am I, O Sovereign LORD, and what is my family, that you have brought me this far?" (2 Sam. 7:18). Not only does he praise God for the blessing of his family but also for the blessings bestowed on Israel. "You have established your people Israel as your very own forever, and you, O LORD, have become their God" (2 Sam. 7:24). David concluded his prayer by asking God for continued blessings on his family. We need to be mindful of God's desire for our life and be aware of His continued blessings.

David continued to conquer the enemies in the land. He was God's warrior, preparing the land and preparing God's people for the time of peace when God would have David's son, Solomon, build the Temple. With peace in the land, the focus of the nation of Israel would be on the construction of the Temple. David recognized this and had a thankful heart.

Even though David sought God's heart, he was still human and tempted by sin. 2 Samuel 11 records David's disobedience that forever changed his family and his life. While David was walking on the roof of his palace one night, he saw Bathsheba bathing. She was the wife of Uriah the Hittite. Scripture states that she was very beautiful (2 Sam. 11:2). A desire for her filled David's heart. After he had his advisors discover who she was, David had Bathsheba summoned to the palace where he slept with her. Later, Bathsheba sent word that she had conceived his child. It was then that David plotted to have Uriah believe the child was his own. But when Uriah would not go home to his wife because he felt an obligation to his fellow warriors, David plotted to have him killed in battle. On David's orders, Bathsheba was then summoned to the palace to be his wife. Sometimes we are so blinded by our own desires that we justify our foolish actions. It took God sending Nathan the prophet to show David that he had sinned before God. David made no excuses; he immediately repented and humbled himself. Even though God forgave him, David still had to live with the consequences of his sin. The Lord commanded, "Now, therefore, the sword will never depart from your house, because you despised me and took the wife of Uriah the Hittite to be your own" (2 Sam. 12:10). One of the consequences was that God allowed the son of David and Bathsheba to die. It would not be his last time of grieving. One son would kill another and animosity would grow between his children. But, the everlasting promise remained through his son, Solomon.

C. Solomon's Reign

Solomon reigned after King David, his father (1 Kings 2:12). It was an era of peace. Solomon loved God. The Bible says that Solomon obeyed God except that he worshiped in the high places (1 Kings 3:3). His worshiping in the high places would eventually be the kingdom's undoing. Still, even though Solomon had shortcomings, God blessed Solomon as He promised David He would. God was keeping His promise that through the line of David, all would be blessed. The blessing began with the promise to Abraham and continued through the line of David to Solomon.

Early in Solomon's reign, God spoke to Solomon in a dream, "Ask for whatever you want me to give you" (1 Kings 3:5). Solomon replied by acknowledging God's kindness and the blessings given to his father, David. He also showed thankfulness to God for inheriting the throne by humbling himself. He knew that he needed wisdom to lead the people of Israel so he asked God for "a discerning heart to govern your people and to distinguish between right and wrong" (1 Kings 3:9). Scripture tells us that God was pleased with Solomon's request (1 Kings 3:10). God responded by blessing Solomon with wisdom that had not been known before that time nor would be known in all the history to follow. The Bible says that God granted wisdom to Solomon that was greater wisdom than anyone had ever had or would have. Because of this blessing, his fame grew (1 Kings 4:29–31). God honors His people when they have a thankful heart and a humble posture.

Just as God had promised David, Solomon built God's Temple. During construction, Solomon demanded holiness for the Temple by maintaining a reverence around the construction. 1 Kings 6:7 states, "In building the temple, only blocks dressed at the quarry were used, and no hammer, chisel or any other iron tool was heard at the temple site while it was being built." He built the Temple exactly to God's specifications, and it was pleasing to the Lord.

After the Temple was built, the Ark of the Covenant was placed in the Most Holy Place by the priest (1 Kings 8:6). God showed His approval by coming down and filling the Temple with His presence (1 Kings 8:10–13). Solomon then prayed for obedience for Israel. "May the LORD our God be with us as he was with our fathers; may he never leave us nor forsake us. May he turn our hearts to him, to walk in all his ways and to keep the commands, decrees and regulations he gave our fathers" (1 Kings 8:57–58). In response, the Lord made a covenant with Solomon (1 Kings 9:3–5). As long as Solomon and his sons walked with God, He would bless them. Then He gave warning, "But if you or your sons turn away from me and do not observe the commands and decrees I have given you and go off to serve other gods and worship them, then I will cut off Israel from the land I have given them and will reject this temple I have consecrated for my Name. Israel will then become a byword and an object of ridicule among all peoples" (1 Kings 9:6–7). It was a stern warning that Solomon should have taken more seriously.

The first part of Solomon's reign, he obeyed God and followed His commands. But with time, Solomon was wooed by the love for his wives, who led him astray to other gods (1 Kings 11:3–4). This angered God. He punished Solomon for his disobedience. "Since this is your attitude and you have not kept my covenant and my decrees, which I commanded you, I will most certainly tear the kingdom away from you and give it to one of your subordinates" (1 Kings 11:11). God remembered His promise to David and told Solomon the kingdom would remain intact until his son took the throne, and for the sake of Jerusalem, God would give his son one tribe to rule (1 Kings 11:12–13). Later we will see that his son's kingdom was a combination of the tribe of Judah and the tribe of Benjamin, also known as the Southern Kingdom of Judah. This kingdom would always have a descendant of David on its throne.

VII. The Divided Kingdom

Before Solomon's death, the division of the kingdom was prophesied by Ahijah the prophet of Shiloh to Jeroboam, one of the officials of Solomon. Meeting Jeroboam at the gates of Jerusalem, the prophet tore his cloak into twelve pieces and handed ten of the pieces to Jeroboam to symbolically show the coming division of the kingdom (1 Kings 11:28–39).

When Solomon died, Rehoboam, his son, succeeded him as king (1 Kings 11:42–43). Then Jeroboam, a representative of the people, went to Rehoboam and asked whether the workload could be lightened because during the time of Solomon, the people worked hard building the Temple and Solomon's palace. Instead of asking God for guidance or listening to his experienced advisors, Rehoboam took council with his young advisors that he had known since childhood. They encouraged him to work the people even harder (1 Kings 12:10–11). Rehoboam took their advice and told the people, "My Father made your yoke heavy; I will make it even heavier. My father scourged you with whips; I will scourge you with scorpions" (1 Kings 12:14). In rebellion to the oppression, the northern tribes crowned Jeroboam as their king and formed the Northern Kingdom of Israel (1 Kings 12:20), also referred to as Samaria (1 Kings 13:32). Rehoboam prepared to attack, but then listened and obeyed God and did not respond to Israel's rebellion (1 Kings 12:21–24). This left the Kingdom divided with Rehoboam as king of the Southern Kingdom of Judah (1 Kings 12:23) just as God had told Solomon.

Jeroboam settled in Shechem in the land of Ephraim but realized quickly that the people of Israel did not have a place to worship (1 Kings 12:26–27). The only place to sacrifice to God was in the Temple in Jerusalem located in the Southern Kingdom of Judah. He feared that the people would turn their allegiance back to Rehoboam and kill him to gain access to the Temple. Therefore, he made two golden calves for the people to worship. He told his people, "It is too much for you to go up to Jerusalem. Here are your gods, O Israel, who brought you up out of Egypt" (1 Kings 12:28). Jeroboam's decision to make a graven image and to turn his people from God eventually led to the nation's destruction. Several prophets, including Hosea, tried to turn the people of the Northern Kingdom of Israel back to God. He warned the Northern Kingdom that they had committed adultery by worshiping other gods. He also prophesied the end of the Northern Kingdom of Israel (Hosea 11:1–7), but the people did not listen. Since they did not repent, God allowed Assyria, one of the most feared empires of ancient times, to conquer the Northern Kingdom (2 Kings 17:4–6). Assyrian tortured their captives ruthlessly. The ones that survived were dispersed over the land of Assyria. Survivors would be weakened, fearful, and submissive, leaving the captured nation stripped of its identity.[7] For the Northern Kingdom, their captivity left them with no place to come together to meet with God. Soon they blended with the people of the Assyrian land. The survivors that remained in the area of Samaria intermarried with the conquering Assyrians and were later referred to in the New Testament as Samaritans. During the years of the New Testament, the Jews (the descendants of the Southern Kingdom of Judah) would have nothing to do with the Samaritans (John 4:9) because they were considered impure from intermarrying with foreigners. Not only did the Jews look down on the Samaritans, but they would not even travel through their land. Instead, they would take the long way and circle around Samaria to travel to the northern region of Mesopotamia.

The Northern Kingdom of Israel was never mentioned again in the Bible as a nation. Because they did not obey God, they lost their identity and their direction. God's plan continued through the Southern Kingdom of Judah.

VIII. The Southern Kingdom of Judah Alone

The nation of Judah had Jerusalem! Having the Temple to communicate with God helped them be brought back into the fold each time they strayed from God's leadership. Note that during the time of the Southern Kingdom, the people of Judah began to be called Judeans (1 Chron. 4:18).

While Judah stood alone, the Babylonian Empire rose to power and crushed the Assyrian Empire. Even though the Babylonians were not as fierce as the Assyrians, they were determined to conquer all the land. King Nebuchadnezzar set his sights on the Southern Kingdom of Judah. The Kingdom was a prime target because they had turned from God and were worshiping other gods. God had sent many prophets to warn the nation of Judah of its impending doom, but they did not listen. Jeremiah spent his life prophesying God's warnings. Finally, God had had enough. Jeremiah changed his words from warnings to prophecy of destruction. Just before the invasion, Jeremiah told the nation of Judah, "Therefore the LORD Almighty says this: 'Because you have not listened to my words, I will summon all the peoples of the north and my servant Nebuchadnezzar king of Babylon,' declares the LORD, 'and I will bring them against this land and its inhabitants and against all the surrounding nations... This whole country will become a desolate wasteland, and these nations will serve the king of Babylon seventy years'" (Jer. 25:8–11). But still, the people of Judah did not repent. Hence, at God's appointed time, God gave the Southern Kingdom of Judah over to be subdued by King Nebuchadnezzar of Babylon (Jer. 39:1). As Jeremiah had prophesied, the Babylonians destroyed the city of Jerusalem and the Temple, Judah's pride and glory.

IX. The Captivity of Judah

During the Babylonian captivity, King Nebuchadnezzar attempted to force the Judeans to worship the Babylonian gods. It was not until God humbled Nebuchadnezzar that he changed his ways and recognized God as the Most High God. "At the end of that time, I, Nebuchadnezzar, raised my eyes toward heaven, and my sanity was restored. Then I praised the Most High; I honored and glorified him who lives forever" (Dan. 4:34). Before this, I have no doubt that the Judeans cried out to God for deliverance as they did in the days of the Judges. They remained under Babylonian control for seventy years as Jeremiah had prophesied (Jer. 25:11). Even though His people were in captivity, God continued to speak through His prophets, Daniel and Ezekiel, encouraging the people to persist and trust in God.

The first five chapters of the book of Daniel record some of the events during the Babylonian captivity. In chapter 2 is recorded Nebuchadnezzar's vision of the statue that Daniel prophesied as the world powers to come. In chapter 3 the familiar story of Shadrach, Meshach, and Abednego being protected by God in the fiery furnace is told. Each event points to God and shows His sovereignty.

When Nebuchadnezzar died, Belshazzar, his son (Dan. 5:2), took the throne. He did not follow the ways of God. During this same time, Cyrus the Great rose to power and led the Persians to defeat the Medes. The joining of these two nations into one increased the strength of the Persian army. Their true power was realized one night when King Belshazzar was giving a "great banquet for a thousand of his nobles" (Dan. 5:1). The Bible tells how during the meal a human hand appeared and started writing on the wall of the banquet hall (Dan. 5:5). "His (King Belshazzar's) face turned pale and he was so frightened that his knees knocked together and his legs gave way" (Dan. 5:6). After none of the enchanters, astrologers, or diviners was able to decipher the words, Daniel was summoned to interpret the mysterious writing. Immediately, Daniel recognized it as prophecy, warning of the end of the Babylonian Empire (Dan. 5:17–28). God wasted no time because that very night, the Mede–Persians toppled the Babylonians and Darius the Mede became the new king of the land (Dan. 5:30–31).

X. The Restoration of Israel

Unlike the Babylonians, the Persians were not as strict with their captives. Isaiah had prophesied that King Cyrus of the Persians would allow the people of God to return to Jerusalem and rebuild the city (Isa. 45:13). In the book of Ezra, we see this prophecy fulfilled.

> *This is what Cyrus king of Persia says:*
> *"The LORD, the God of heaven, has given me all the kingdoms of the earth and he has appointed me to build a temple for him at Jerusalem in Judah. Anyone of his people among you—may his God be with him, and let him go up to Jerusalem in Judah and build the temple of the LORD, the God of Israel, the God who is in Jerusalem. And the people of any place where survivors may now be living are to provide him with silver and gold, with goods and livestock, and with freewill offerings for the temple of God in Jerusalem"* (Ezra 1:2–4).

Many of the Judeans chose not to return to Jerusalem. The Bible tells of one who remained that God used in a mighty way. Esther, a young Jewish woman who became queen of Persia, saved the entire population of the Jews from annihilation (the book of Esther). God was at work even with the people who chose not to return.

The book of Ezra is devoted to the rebuilding of the Temple and the restoration of the remnant of Israel. The Bible says that after the Israelites had been back in the land for seven months settling in their towns, the Israelites came together to begin work on the Temple. Jeshua the priest (Ezra 3:8) and Zerubbabel the governor of Judah

(Hag. 2:2) led in the building of the foundation of the Temple (Ezra 3:1–2). When the foundation was complete, the people celebrated with shouts of praise and cries of tears in remembrance of the former Temple. The Bible says that the sound of the celebration was heard a great distance away (Ezra 3:8–13)

Unfortunately, completing the work on the Temple was not an easy task. Enemies of the people of Israel caused enough problems to have the then King of Persia, Artaxerxes, order a halt to the construction (Ezra 4:21). It was not until the second year of the reign of King Darius of Persia that the construction continued when Haggai and Zechariah, the prophets, came and encouraged the people to finish the building of the Temple. Haggai told the people that they had become more interested in building their own homes and cities than in restoring the Temple to worship God (Hag. 1:3–11). The people listened to the prophets and began working again on the Temple. When King Darius was told that the rebuilding had begun, he made a decree that the Temple be completed as King Cyrus had commanded years early. Several years later, Nehemiah returned to help rebuild the wall around Jerusalem (Neh. 2:17–18). But the restoration of the city did not mean the full restoration of the people. Even with the history of captivity and the presence of the Temple, the people still fell away from God's commands.

Many years later, Ezra, a priest and teacher of the Law, came from Babylon to Jerusalem (Ezra 7:16). After arriving with other priests and Levites, he learned that the people had not kept the laws but had intermarried with people from other nations (Ezra 9:1–2). Immediately, Ezra prayed to the Lord for forgiveness (Ezra 9:5–15). The Bible says that as Ezra prayed and wept bitterly and threw himself down outside the Temple a crowd gathered around him. As they listened to Ezra's prayers for forgiveness, the people recognized their sin and asked for his leadership to guide them (Ezra 10:1–4). Over the next several days, the people repented of their foreign marriages. A list of the heads of families that had descendants who had intermarried with foreign nations was even brought before the Lord for forgiveness (Ezra 10:18–43). But unfortunately, man cannot stay obedient on his own. The remnant of Israel, God's chosen people, continued to sin.

The book of Malachi is considered by most scholars as the last book of the Old Testament to be penned. He sent a message to the Jews from God: "Return to me, and I will return to you" (Mal. 3:7). In his writings, he addresses two groups of people: the people that have robbed God by not being obedient to God's commands (Mal. 3:8) and the faithful ones that fear God and honor him (Mal. 3:16–18). He tells the people that God will remember the faithful and they will be His, but the disobedient will be consumed by fire (Mal. 4:1–2).

Malachi also prophesies in his writings about coming of John the Baptist. He wrote that the Lord Almighty said, "See, I will send my messenger, who will prepare the way before me. Then suddenly the Lord you are seeking will come to his temple; the messenger of the covenant, whom you desire, will come" (Mal. 3:1). But the people did not listen. The Jews regretted not listening to God's prophets because four hundred years of silence began after Malachi penned God's final words in the Old Testament. God had always spoken to His People. God was still at work, but during the silent years, no Word was heard. No prophets were raised up. God was silent.

Between the Testaments

During the four hundred years between the testaments known as the silent years, the Jews lived through various experiences and challenges that greatly affected them. The Old Testament story ends with Jerusalem restored but obedience to God lagging. The New Testament story begins on the other extreme with religious piety on every street corner. Strict adherence to the laws of Moses was demanded by the religious leaders, along with additional oral laws to ensure obedience to God. Four hundred years had swung the pendulum from negligence of God's law to stringent obedience. Both sides needed a savior.

During the silent years, the Greeks conquered the Persians and took possession of the Jews. Although the Jews were allowed to worship God in their traditional ways, many were Hellenized by incorporating into their Jewish practice the worship of Greek gods. When Antiochus IV became king, he was furious that not all Jews accepted the Hellenistic way of life, so he passed strict laws forbidding the Jews from practicing their religion. In hopes of gaining control of the Jews, he destroyed the Hebrew Scriptures, and anyone caught following Jewish customs was strictly punished[8]. To further disrupt the Jews' worship of God, Antiochus IV tore down the city walls of Jerusalem and set up an idol of Jupiter on the Temple altar and there sacrificed pigs during heathen rituals.[9] Daniel had prophesied this action in Daniel 11:31 when he said, "His armed forces will rise up to desecrate the temple fortress and will abolish the daily sacrifice. Then they will set up the abomination that causes desolation." Because the Temple was desecrated, the Jews were a people without connection to God. Their worship was inhibited.

In 167 B.C., Mattathias, a Jewish priest, outraged by Antiochus IV's actions, led a revolt against the new rulers of Jerusalem. This was the start of the Maccabean Revolt. When he died, his son Judas took the lead and won the rebellion in 165 B.C. He reclaimed Jerusalem and the Temple for the Jews. The Temple was cleansed and rededicated. This victory and rededication of the Temple is the origin of the Feast of Lights or Hanukkah that is celebrated by the Jews to this day. Years later, the Romans conquered the Greeks and placed Herod the Great on the throne in Jerusalem. He renovated the Temple to gain favor with the Jews. This same Herod was the king during the time of Jesus' birth that ordered the death of all males under the age of two in Bethlehem.[10]

Even though terrible things happened to the Jews during the silent years, two significant accomplishments occurred. The Greek language was introduced to the empire to unify the kingdom during the reign of Alexander the Great[11] and the Romans built roads to make travel easier throughout the kingdom.[12] God later used these two achievements to help spread the Good News of Jesus Christ to the uttermost parts of the earth.

The New Testament

I was recently reading through the book of Leviticus and was thanking God with every word that I did not live in a time in which the Levitical Law was necessary to have a relationship with God. Just as the Israelites did, I would have struggled to follow all the rules and regulations. My backyard would have been filled with animals prepared to be sacrificed for my disobedience. During Old Testament times, without a perfect sacrifice, the constant flow of animal blood sacrifice was all this world had to offer to maintain a relationship with God. But those lambs, pigeons, and bulls were only temporary sacrifices because they were not a true, perfect sacrifice (Heb. 10:1–4). The problem—they were not us. But Jesus was. He was God in human flesh. The Bible says, "For in Christ all the fullness of the Deity lives in bodily form" (Col. 2:9). He had the same temptations, but He did not yield. The Bible says, "For we do not have a high priest who is unable to sympathize with our weaknesses, but we have one who has been tempted in every way, just as we are—yet was without sin" (Heb. 4:15). Jesus came to be our perfect sacrifice because He was a man without sin. Therein lies the glory of the New Testament. The Bible says, "God made him who had no sin to be sin for us, so that in him we might become the righteousness of God" (2 Cor. 5:21). "We have been made holy through the sacrifice of the body of Jesus Christ once for all" (Heb. 10:10). The Old Testament was *our* best attempt at perfection. The New Testament is God's perfect plan fulfilled. I am so glad God did not depend on us to find a way to Him. Thankfully, Jesus came down to us and made a way to God.

The New Testament brings hope and redemption to mankind—the provision for sin. It tells the story of Jesus, and then spends the rest of the message telling us how to be more like Christ because the acceptance of salvation is only the beginning of a relationship with God. After we accept Him, we need to learn the instructions God gave us on how to live the abundant life—the best life possible for each one of us. And in that abundant life, the blessings come in being involved in helping God with His continued work on this earth.

XI. Life of Christ

No prophets. No visions. No voices in the wilderness. Just silence. And then without warning, God spoke. At the beginning of the Old Testament, His powerful voice brought creation into existence. But in the New Testament, God's first message was to only one man. "Do not be afraid" (Luke 1:13). As Zacharias stood before the Ark of the Covenant for the yearly cleansing of the people, an angel appeared to him with the first message from God in more than four hundred years. The angel told Zacharias that he and his wife, Elizabeth, were to have a son and to name him John. "He will be filled with the Holy Spirit even from birth. Many of the people of Israel will he bring back to the Lord their God. And he will go on before the Lord, in the spirit and power of Elijah, to turn the hearts of the fathers to their children and the disobedient to the wisdom of the righteous—to make ready a people prepared for the Lord" (Luke 1:15–17). Just as Elijah preached repentance in the Old Testament, John, also known as John the Baptist, was given this same boldness to preach repentance to the people of the New Testament. The Bible says, "And the child grew and became strong in the spirit; and he lived in the desert until he appeared publicly to Israel" (Luke 1:80). God used John's powerful gift of boldness to prepare the way for the coming of the Messiah.

Before the Messiah, God's Son, was introduced to the world, He came into the world as flesh and blood through a virgin named Mary (Luke 1:34–35). All of Heaven must have been on the edge of its seat because once God spoke, they knew the time was near for the Savior of the world to be born. The anticipation must have been overwhelming. When the time came, instead of shouting His

Son's birth on the mountain tops to the world or through the inner throne rooms to the kings of nations, God chose to celebrate His Son's birth with some lowly shepherds in a field (Luke 2:8–18). God's Son, Jesus, was not born into this world to establish an earthly kingdom to be served, but instead, He came to be a savior to sinners (Luke 5:32). The shepherds watched in amazement at the heavenly celebration! The night sky lit up! "A great company of the heavenly host appeared with the angel praising God and saying, 'Glory to God in the highest, and on earth peace to men on whom his favor rests'" (Luke 2:13–14). After the angels went back into heaven, I can only imagine the shepherds' excitement as they hurried to Bethlehem to see the Christ child. There in a stable, the shepherds came face to face with their Messiah. Did they fall down in worship or stand in awe at the baby who lay before them? I do know. It had to be a meeting filled with anticipation and much excitement. As night gave way to dawn, the Bible says that the shepherds left the manger telling everyone who would listen about the wondrous sight that they had witnessed (Luke 2:17). God's timing was perfect because the streets of Bethlehem were filled with travelers that had come for the census (Luke 2:1–3). Those same travelers later returned to their hometowns and shared all they had heard on the streets of Bethlehem about the Christ child's birth. This allowed the news of the Messiah's birth to spread quickly.

It was not long until King Herod heard the news. His reaction was not one of praise and adoration but of fear and jealousy. Herod was afraid that if Jesus was the Messiah, He would one day set up His kingdom and remove him from power. The king tried to kill the Christ child by murdering every male two years and under in Bethlehem (Matt. 2:16), but God protected Jesus by warning His earthly father, Joseph, to take the child to Egypt to stay until the danger passed (Matt. 2:13). After Herod died, an angel again visited Joseph and told him that his family could return home (Matt. 2:19–20). But once they had begun their journey, Joseph was warned in a dream to go to the town of Nazareth and live because Archelaus, the son of Herod, had taken the throne. So, Jesus spent his childhood and adolescent years living in the city of Nazareth (Matt. 2:22–23). The Bible says, "Jesus grew in wisdom and stature, and in favor with God and man" (Luke 2:52).

Little is mentioned in the Bible about Jesus's childhood and young adult years. Born a Jew, the Bible does tells us that He was circumcised at eight days old and presented to the Temple in accordance with Jewish custom (Luke 2:21–38). At age twelve, we read that Jesus traveled with his parents for the Feast of Passover in Jerusalem (Luke 2:41–42). When his parents began the journey home, they realized that their son was not with them. After a three day search, Jesus was found in the Temple among the teachers asking them questions and listening intently to what they had to say (Luke 2:46). When asked by His parents why He had caused them to worry, Jesus's responded, "Why were you searching for me? Didn't you know I had to be in my Father's house?" (Luke 2:49). This is the first time in Scripture where we learn that Jesus knew His Father. The greatest concentration given to Jesus's life is His three years of ministry. Many things about His life are not recorded in the Scriptures. In the Gospel of John, the apostle wrote that most of the events in Jesus's life were not recorded because "if every one of them were written down, I suppose that even the whole world would not have room for the books that would be written" (John 21:25). So what was recorded, God deemed most important to mankind.

The Bible records that when Jesus was about thirty years old, he began his ministry (Luke 3:23). By this time, John, better known as John the Baptist, was already on the scene, preparing the world for Jesus's entrance. "In those days John the Baptist came, preaching in the Desert of Judea and saying, 'Repent, for the kingdom of heaven is near'" (Matt. 3:1–2). He preached this to anyone who would listen.

> *I baptize you with water for repentance. But after me will come one who is more powerful than I, whose sandals I am not fit to carry. He will baptize you with*

> the Holy Spirit and with fire. His winnowing fork is in his hand, and he will clear his threshing floor, gathering his wheat into the barn and burning up the chaff with unquenchable fire
> (Matt. 3:11–12).

Jesus's ministry began when John baptized Him in the Jordan River. It was then that God introduced His Son to the world. The Bible says, "As soon as Jesus was baptized, he went up out of the water. At that moment heaven was opened, and he saw the Spirit of God descending like a dove and lighting on him. And a voice from heaven said, 'This is my Son, whom I love; with him I am well pleased'" (Matt. 3:16–17). After this, Jesus went into the desert to be tempted by Satan (Matt. 4:1–11). Each time He was tempted, He quoted God's words, which gave Him the strength to avoid sinning. His example shows us the importance of hiding God's word in our heart where we too can avoid the snares of Satan (Ps. 119:11).

Jesus's ministry was short-lived but filled with much activity. In those three years, He spent every moment doing the will of His Father. Jesus said, "For I have come down from heaven not to do my will but to do the will of him who sent me" (John 6:38).

The purpose of Jesus's ministry was threefold. First, He came to tell the world about His Father. This was accomplished through preaching and teaching and performing miracles. Second, He came to reflect the character of God. Jesus told Philip, one of the disciples, "Anyone who has seen me has seen the Father" (John 14:9). Not only did He live a sinless life (Heb. 4:15), but He lived a life filled with compassion and love for all people. But most importantly, Jesus came to die on the cross to pay the ultimate price for our sins, revealing the love and forgiveness of His Father.

Throughout His ministry, Jesus performed numerous miracles. Some were healing miracles that involved making the lame to walk and the blind to see. There are even three miracles mentioned in the Bible where Jesus raised the dead (Matt. 9:18–19, 23–26; Luke

7:11–17; John 11:1–44). But not all of His miracles involved healing. Many were miracles that dealt with nature like calming the storm while out on the Sea of Galilee with His disciples (Matt. 8:23–27) and feeding a crowd of five thousand with only five loaves of bread and two fish (Matt. 14:15–21). These were to show God in control of His creation. God not only created but sustains creation. These wonders not only caught the people's attention, but showed God's power and compassion. Even when performing miracles, Jesus's focus was always directed toward the Father.

Not only did Jesus show who God is through miracles He performed, but He also revealed who God is by His teaching and preaching to all who would listen. As He traveled, He could be found in the synagogues, on the city streets, or at the water's edge telling others about His Father. His desire was for all to come to know the truth (1 Tim. 2:3–4). Because of this, He rarely stayed long in one place. This is emphasized in Mark 1:38–39 after Jesus had preached and healed many in the town of Capernaum: "Jesus replied, 'Let us go somewhere else—to the nearby villages—so I can preach there also. That is why I have come.' So he traveled throughout Galilee, preaching in their synagogues and driving out demons." When Jesus came to a city, He would search out the synagogue and teach whenever possible.

On several occasions, Jesus was confronted by individuals who were demon-possessed. The power and authority of God were revealed because the evil spirits had no choice but to obey His voice. At times, they even called out His name. In Capernaum, where Jesus was teaching in the synagogue, a man "possessed by an evil spirit cried out, 'What do you want with us, Jesus of Nazareth? Have you come to destroy us? I know who you are—the Holy One of God!'" (Mark 1:23–24). Jesus rebuked the spirit and commanded, "Be quiet! Come out of him!" (Mark 1:25). Scripture states, "The evil spirit shook the man violently and came out of him with a shriek" (Mark 1:26). Christ did not want nor need the testimony of demons to proclaim who He was. People were amazed at Jesus's authority.

His words could quiet the demons, His touch could heal the sick, and His presence could give hope to the weary. The crowds clamored to see Him while the news of His presence spread, causing more people to seek Him.

Sometimes the crowds were so great that Jesus would find a place outside the city gates to do His preaching. On one occasion, Jesus went up on a mountainside near the Sea of Galilee to speak to the crowd that had gathered. This event quickly came to be known as the "Sermon on the Mount." Many consider this to be one of Jesus's greatest sermons during His ministry. In these words that Matthew recorded in three chapters of his book, Jesus shares that the attitude of the believer is as important as his or her own actions (Matt. 5–7). The heart of a person determines how God can use them to further His work, and the more a person is used, the more abundant his life becomes. Jesus also pointed out in His sermon that He did not come to abolish the Law but to fulfill it (Matt. 5:17). Here lies an important truth for the believer. Because Jesus lived a perfect life, He lived a life that met the requirements of the Law. And because He met the requirements of the Law, He could die for our sins. Therefore, anyone who accepts Jesus as their Savior is not bound to the Law because Jesus's gift of sacrifice replaces the penalty of the Law. As Scripture states, "I have not come to abolish them" (Matt. 5:17), the Law remains for the judgment of those who choose not to follow Christ. For the believer, the Law becomes the guiding principle for living the abundant life. Though the people did not understand all that the Savior said, they hung on His every Word and sought understanding in His message. But it was not long until those same crowds would turn against Him and demand His crucifixion (Luke 23:21).

The times in which I see Jesus's heart the most is when He spoke to a small group or when he spoke one-on-one with an individual. For example, there are many stories of Jesus sharing moments alone with three disciples: Peter, James, and John, often considered the inner circle. They witnessed Jesus's transfiguration when Moses and Elijah appeared (Luke 9:28–36). They witnessed the healing of Jairus's daughter (Luke 8:40–42, 49–56). They, alone, were privy to Jesus's troubled heart in the Garden of Gethsemane the day before His crucifixion (Matt. 26:37–38). Then there were times when Jesus spoke one-on-one with individuals. With Zacchaeus, Jesus visited with him in his home (Luke 19:1–10). The woman at the well, He filled her with living water (John 4:4–30, 39–42). Then there was the woman that touched the hem of His garment; He healed her immediately (Luke 8:42–48). No matter if Jesus was in a crowd or one-on-one, He had compassion and shared the love that came from His Father.

The ultimate reason that Christ came to earth was to pay the penalty for our sins. John 3:16 states, "For God so loved the world that he gave his one and only Son, that whoever believes in him shall not perish but have eternal life." Christ's life was meant for the cross from the day He was born. He came to be our sacrifice "once for all when he offered himself" (Heb. 7:27). He is the provision for our sin that is first mentioned in Genesis 3:15 when God spoke to the serpent: "And I will put enmity between you and the woman, and between your offspring and hers; he will crush your head, and you will strike his heel." Yes, sin caused Jesus much pain on the cross, but by His death, Jesus was victorious over sin and paid sin's penalty for all who would accept His gift of salvation.

The story of Jesus's life does not end in the grave. On the third day, the Lord's Day, Jesus rose from the grave to be our living God (1 Cor. 15:4) to ultimately defeat death and reign with His Father forever (Heb. 1:8)! In Revelations, Jesus states, "Do not be afraid. I am the First and the Last. I am the Living One; I was dead, and behold I am alive for ever and ever! And I hold the keys of death and Hades" (Rev. 1:17–18). We serve a living God! A loving God! A God who understands and can sympathize with our every need (Heb. 4:15). God so wanted a relationship with us that His plan that was revealed in the Garden was fulfilled by His One and only Son on the cross on a lonely hill in Jerusalem. With every turn and twist of the journey to the cross, God protected His plan and His people. A famine during the time of Jacob, enslavement by the Egyptians, captivity by the Babylonians that took them from their land, a threat of annihilation by Haman's plot in the book of Esther, Antiochus Epiphanes's plot to destroy the Jews, and the constant disobedience of God's people did not keep Jesus from the cross. The Bible says, "Many are the plans in a man's heart, but it is the LORD's purpose that prevails" (Prov. 19:21). Thank goodness, God's plan did not rely on mankind, but on the perfect love of God.

In Him we have life and that life sets us free from death. After being seen for over a period of forty days on this earth, Jesus ascended into heaven to be with his Father (Acts 1:9). And one day, we will be with Him. When I think of Heaven, I think of the Garden of Eden. It was perfect. I believe it was a foreshadowing of things to come. With Satan locked away in the eternal lake of fire (Rev. 20:10), there will be no serpent to tempt (Rev. 22:3). So there will be no sorrow or sadness. We will be made whole. Jesus says in Revelation that when we get to Heaven, we will eat of the Tree of Life and live forever with God in Paradise (Rev. 2:7). What a day that will be when we can truly get the complete *big picture*! It will be fun filling in the picture with the One True God who made it!

XII. The Establishment of the Early Church

The book of Acts is the final history book of the Bible, briefly covering the birth of the church, which is the beginning of the establishment of believers. Before Christ ascended to Heaven, He gave the great commission that commanded believers to share the Gospel with the uttermost parts of the world (Matt. 28:18–20). This was possible by the indwelling of the Holy Spirit that guided believers and gave them courage to go beyond the walls of Jerusalem and reach all people for Christ.

The book of Acts can be broken down into four main parts: the period of waiting for the Holy Spirit, the time of Pentecost, the persecution, and the spread of the Gospel. When Jesus ascended into Heaven, God did not leave His people alone to do His work. He had a plan, and He guided them personally each step of the way.

A. The Period of Waiting for the Holy Spirit

The story of Acts begins at the end of the forty-day period that Jesus was seen after His resurrection (Acts 1:3). Before Jesus ascended into Heaven, Acts records that He told His disciples not to leave Jerusalem but to wait. "Do not leave Jerusalem, but wait for the gift my Father promised, which you have heard me speak about. For John baptized with water, but in a few days you will be baptized with the Holy Spirit" (Acts 1:4–5; see John 14:16). I am certain they had no idea what He was talking about, but they were committed to obedience. So when Jesus ascended to His Father, the disciples gathered in an upper room and awaited the arrival (Acts 1:12–14).

B. The Time of Pentecost

"Suddenly a sound like the blowing of a violent wind came from heaven and filled the whole house where they were sitting" (Acts 2:2). What an experience that must have been! God's gift was more than a pretty package wrapped in a big red bow. It was a part of God Himself—His Spirit—in full power and glory anointing all the believers. The last time the Spirit of God descended on a man was when He came down in the form of a dove and rested on Jesus, Himself. Though God spoke then, this time His mere presence had the elements of nature stirred up and roaring for all to hear. "They saw what seemed to be tongues of fire that separated and came to rest on each of them. All of them were filled with the Holy Spirit and began to speak in other tongues as the Spirit enabled them" (Acts 2:3–4). The Bible says that not only the believers witnessed the Spirit's arrival, but the crowds that lined the streets of Jerusalem for the Pentecost festival also heard and gathered around the house to see what was happening. The Spirit enabled the people to hear in their own tongue the message from God that was being delivered by the believers (Acts 2:6).

God's Spirit did not just stir up the winds, it shook souls. The Bible says that Peter was moved with boldness as he stood in the midst of the crowd, preaching the Gospel with power and conviction. "Therefore let all Israel be assured of this: God has made this Jesus, whom you crucified, both Lord and Christ" (Acts 2:36). After he had finished, the people were moved in their hearts by the Spirit and asked Peter for direction. He responded, "Repent and be baptized, every one of you, in the name of Jesus Christ for the forgiveness of your sins. And you will receive the gift of the Holy Spirit. The promise is for you and your children and for all who are far off—for all whom the Lord our God will call" (Acts 2:38–39). From that day forward, the gift of the Holy Spirit indwells all believers to teach and to remind us of who God is (John 14:26). What a precious gift to have a part of God living inside each of us.

On the day of Pentecost, the Bible says that 3000 people accepted Jesus as their Savior and were baptized (Acts 2:41). The believers bonded together and stayed in Jerusalem, while their numbers grew daily (Acts 2:42–47). But remember, God wanted the Gospel to be spread beyond the walls of Jerusalem to the uttermost parts of the earth (Matt. 28:18–20). This was accomplished by persecution of the believers in Jerusalem.

C. *The Persecution*

The disciples had witnessed the life, death, and resurrection of Jesus Christ. They might have been content to stay within the walls of Jerusalem, but they could not help but leave their homes and pour into the city streets to share with all of Jerusalem the gift of salvation from God. This outpouring was the tool God used to push the Christians beyond the walls of their comfort zone. The Jewish leaders feared this divine boldness would cause Rome to squelch a perceived rebellion, possibly stripping them of their positions as leaders over the Jewish people. They had breathed a sigh of relief when Jesus was put to death, but now they feared His followers would finish the work they thought Jesus had begun. Unfortunately, they were so preoccupied with the possibility of losing their status that they missed the true message of salvation. To stop the uprising, the Jewish leaders started persecuting the Christians.

The persecution began with the arrest of Peter and John for claiming to heal a crippled man by the power of the resurrected Lord (Acts 4:1–2). The Sanhedrin, the Jewish council, wanted to hold them, but because they could see the healed man before their eyes, they had no grounds to keep them imprisoned. So, they warned them to no longer speak in the name of Jesus before they set them free. Peter and John refused to be silent. They could not deny the salvation of the risen Lord.

The intensity of the Christian movement grew as more people witnessed their sick family members and friends being healed in the name of Jesus and heard the life-changing Word of God. The Bible says that the high priest, captain of the guard, and the Sadducees were greatly distressed about Peter and John "teaching the people and proclaiming in Jesus the resurrection of the dead" (Acts 4:2). To add to the troubles, the Sadducees did not believe in an afterlife, so they had them arrested again and thrown into prison. This time in the middle of the night, God sent an angel to open the cell doors and lead them out to safety (Acts 5:18–19). Once freed, the angel commanded them to return to the Temple and continue telling the people about Jesus. Soon, the Sanhedrin realized their absence. When they were found in the Temple courts teaching, they were again brought before the Sanhedrin. The court questioned why they had continued to preach in the name of Jesus. The council voiced their biggest fear when they said, "Yet you have filled Jerusalem with your teaching and are determined to make us guilty of this man's blood" (Acts 5:28). Peter and his associates responded boldly by saying,

> *We must obey God rather than men! The God of our fathers raised Jesus from the dead—whom you had killed by hanging him on a tree. God exalted him to his own right hand as Prince and Savior that he might give repentance and forgiveness of sins to Israel. We are witnesses of these things, and so is the Holy Spirit, whom God has given to those who obey him* (Acts 5:29–32).

The council was angered by Peter's testimony and wanted to put Peter and John to death because of the attention they were receiving. But Gamaliel, one of the teachers of the Law, cautioned the Sanhedrin that the deaths of Peter and John might cause the movement to grow in strength because they would be considered martyrs for the cause. So instead, they flogged them both and sent them on their way with more warnings not to speak about Jesus, which they refused (Acts 5:34–40). Each time persecution came, the Word of God spread and more people joined the body of Christ.

The first martyr for the Christian faith was Stephen. He had angered members of the synagogue because God had filled him with wisdom that they could not dispute (Acts 6:10). They found men who would falsely accuse him of blasphemy against Moses and against God. When he was brought before the Sanhedrin to be accused, everyone saw "his face was like the face of angel" (Acts 6:15). As Stephen stood before the council, the high priest asked him if the charges were true. Stephen answered with one of the most powerful speeches found in the Bible. His words are a summary of the events that occurred to the Israelites from the time that

God called Abraham out of Mesopotamia to the time of Solomon's Temple. He went on to tell them that they put to death prophets that prophesied Jesus's coming. Then Stephen was bold and accused the Sanhedrin of murdering the Messiah (Acts 7:52). When they heard this, they were furious. "But Stephen, full of the Holy Spirit, looked up to heaven and saw the glory of God, and Jesus standing at the right hand of God. 'Look,' he said, 'I see heaven open and the Son of Man standing at the right hand of God" (Acts 7:55–56). At this, they dragged him outside the city walls and stoned him (Acts 7:58). This event caused all the believers, except the apostles, to flee the city and scatter throughout Judea and Samaria (Acts 8:1).

During the stoning of Stephen, Saul is introduced to the story. He was the man who held the coats of the accusers when they stoned Stephen (Acts 7:58). After the stoning, the Bible says that Saul began destroying the churches and throwing all the followers of Jesus that he could find into prison (Acts 8:3). It was a terrible time of persecution.

One day when Saul was on the road to Damascus to persecute more believers, God revealed Himself to Saul.

> *As he neared Damascus on his journey, suddenly a light from heaven flashed around him. He fell to the ground and heard a voice say to him, "Saul, Saul, why do you persecute me?"*
> *"Who are you, Lord?" Saul asked.*
> *"I am Jesus, whom you are persecuting," he replied.*
> *"Now get up and go into the city, and you will be told what you must do"* (Acts 9:3–6).

The Bible continues by saying that Jesus told Saul to go into Damascus and find a man named Ananias. Saul obeyed, but when he got up, he realized he was blind so he had to be guided into Damascus. Not surprisingly, his fellow travelers were stunned because they heard God's voice but did not see Him. With the help of Ananias the prophet, Saul gained his sight back and with it a new found faith in Jesus Christ. In his remaining years, Saul spent his time telling anyone who would listen about the saving power of Jesus Christ. Possibly because God called Saul to preach to the Gentiles, Luke, the author of Acts, eventually started calling Saul by his Greek name, Paul (Acts 13:9).

D. The Spread of the Gospel

The Bible says that after the death of Stephen, the believers fled "as far as Phoenicia, Cyprus and Antioch, telling the message only to the Jews" (Acts 11:19). Some continued on to Cyprus and shared the Gospel with the Greeks (Acts 11:20). But, for the most part during this time, the Gospel was being shared only with the Jews. Remember John 3:16, "For God so loved the world..." Jesus tells us through these words that salvation was meant for all people, but the majority of Jews, God's chosen people, had spent centuries believing that they were the only ones blessed by God. Many of God's people did not realize that the promise of the blessing given to Abraham and his descendants was for all people. This revelation did not become clear to the believing Jews until Peter had a vision in which God showed him that salvation was for all (Acts 11:4–18). With this revelation, the Gospel began to spread to all people. Paul felt convicted to witness to the Gentiles, while Peter continued preaching the gospel to the Jews (Gal. 2:7). The remainder of Acts is filled with stories of these and others as they spread the gospel to all the world.

Today, it has been more than 2,000 years since our Savior lived on the earth, but our mission is still the same as it was for Peter and Paul and all the apostles. Our work is to continue to spread the story of Jesus and His saving grace. The Gospel of Matthew shares with all believers this great commission, given by Jesus on the Mount of Olives before He returned to His Father.

> *All authority in heaven and on earth has been given to me. Therefore go and make disciples of all nations, baptizing them in the name of the Father and of the Son and of the Holy Spirit, and teaching them to obey everything I have commanded you. And surely I am with you always, to the very end of the age* (Matt. 28:18–20).

It truly is an exciting story. The God of the universe loved His creation so much that He gave His Son to die on an old rugged cross that we all might have a relationship with Him. Truly we serve a living, a loving God. It is the story of the Bible—a message of love from God to you.

---

1. Moore, Beth. *Believing God*. Nashville, Tenn.: Lifeway Press, 2014. 42.
2. Parke, Ph.D, Ivan. E–mail interview by author. March 21, 2015.
3. Hicks, Laurel. "The Fertile Crescent: Cradle of Civilization." In *Old World History & Geography in Christian Perspective*. 3rd ed. Pensacola, Fla.: A Beka Book, 2008. 66–75.
4. Horton, Beka. *Genesis—First Things*. Pensacola, Fla.: A Beka Book., 1997. 120–21.
5. Butler, Trent C. "Sanhedrin" In *Holman Bible Dictionary: With Summary Definitions and Explanatory Articles on Every Bible Subject, Introductions and Teaching Outlines for Each Bible Book, In–depth Theological Articles, plus Internal Maps, Charts, Illustrations, Scale Reconstruction Drawings, Archaeological Photos, and Atlas*. Nashville, TN: Holman Bible Publishers, 1991.

6. Scofield, C. I., ed., "The Book of 1 Samuel" In *The Scofield Study Bible: New International Version*. [Red Letter Ed.], New York: Oxford University Press, 2004. 8:5.
7. Mark, Joshua J. "Assyrian Warfare." Ancient History Encyclopedia. August 11, 2014. Accessed March 26, 2015. http://www.ancient.eu/Assyrian_Warfare/.
8. Halley, Henry Hampton. *Halley's Bible Handbook with the New International Version*. 25th ed. Grand Rapids, Mich.: Zondervan, 2000. 508
9. Josephus, Flavius, and William Whiston. "The Antiquities of the Jews, XII.5.4." In *The Works of Josephus: Complete and Unabridged*. New Updated ed. Peabody, MA: Hendrickson Publishers, 1987. 324.
10. Halley, Henry Hampton. *Halley's Bible Handbook with the New International Version*. 25th ed. Grand Rapids, Mich.: Zondervan, 2000. 508–511.
11. Sleeth, Naomi, ed. *Old World History and Geography: In Christian Perspective*. 3rd ed. Pensacola, Fla.: A Beka Book, 2008. 231.
12. Ibid, 238.

Recognizing the Message

Now that you have studied the basic skeleton from the Garden of Eden to the cross and beyond, did you understand God's message? Did you see how the stories connect together to show how God desires to have a relationship with each one of us? Remember how man's relationship with God was broken in the Garden of Eden by sin? To again have that relationship, man needed a payment for his sin. But death and separation from God was the only true payment (Rom. 6:23). So, to live with God, man needed a substitute. The animal sacrifices of the Old Testament temporarily covered sin (Heb. 10:1–4), but God wanted us to live with Him in eternity. The only way for this to be accomplished was to have a perfect human sacrificed as payment for man's sin. Jesus was a man, but without sin. He was that perfect sacrifice (Heb. 10:11–12). He died for our sins "so that in him we might become the righteousness of God" (2 Cor. 5:21). "Now he has reconciled you by Christ's physical body through death to present you holy in his sight, without blemish and free from accusation" (Col. 1:22). When we accept the gift of salvation, we accept Jesus's payment for our sin. This gift makes us holy and brings us back into fellowship with God for eternity!

Beginning with Genesis 3:15, which introduced the need for a provision for man's sin, to Seth to Noah to Abraham to Joseph to Rahab to Esther to the cross, God's desire for a relationship with you and me becomes clear. The Gospel of John seals this message by making it personal (John 3:16). John called himself "the one Jesus loved" (John 20:2) or "the disciple whom Jesus loved" (John 21:20). It might sound selfish at first read, but look deeper into John's message. John recognized that God loves each one of us individually for who we are. God's love for each of us is unique, creating a personal relationship with Him. God declared to Jeremiah, "For I know the plans I have for you, plans to prosper you and not to harm you, plans to give you hope and a future" (Jer. 29:11). Personal. God wants every person to know Him (1 Tim. 2:3–4). In the last history book of the Bible, Acts, God emphasizes His desire that all would know Him because He sent His Spirit to indwell believers to enable each believer to tell others about Him (Acts 1:8).

Each story of the Bible connects together to share this unbelievable love God has for each one of us. It is a beautiful love letter from God to you. We serve a living God, a loving God—the God who loves you.

Now It Is Your Turn to Do the Digging

I have expanded those thirteen original pages to just over hundred pages for you. Still, you hold in your hands only a brief outline of the Bible. Do not be overwhelmed by the massive information that is left to dig. My suggestion is to use the *Guide for Reading the History of the Bible* (see page 117) located in the appendix to read through the history of the Bible. This will reinforce the twelve historical periods that we have studied and help prepare you for future studies and personal digs. Ask for God to reveal Himself in His Word. Do not be surprised when you find Him everywhere your eyes look. He is on every page, in every word, waiting for you to find Him. The Bible says, "You will seek me and find me when you seek me with all your heart" (Jer. 29:13). I love that He is always waiting to reveal more of Himself to us. Now it is your turn. Enjoy your dig in the Bible, and when you can, bring a friend along to the site.

Appendix

*Study to shew thyself approved unto God,
a workman that needeth not to be ashamed,
rightly dividing the word of truth*
(2 Timothy 2:15, KJV).

From Me to You

In this appendix, I prepared some very helpful aids. First, I have inserted three of my most treasured charts that I have created. These give, at first glance, an understanding of how the Bible is organized and the chronological order of its history. A copy of all three of them I keep folded in my Bible as a reference guide. Second, there is a brief summary of each of the history books to give you a quick glance of what is found in each book. Finally, I have prepared a guide for reading through the history of the Bible to obtain the story of the Bible or what I like to call the *big picture*. It is easy to become overwhelmed with the magnitude and complexity of Scripture. This reading guide pulls out the main story line and gives you a quick overview, which will help you better grasp the skeleton of the Bible. I highly suggest that you use an easy reading Bible to obtain this overview. *The Living Bible* or *Children's Bible: English Standard Version* are perfect choices for reading through the Bible without the complexity of wording or difficulty in syntax. If you have never read through the Bible with one of these simpler versions, you will be surprised how much you enjoy reading and how much more of the message that you will comprehend. When you are ready to study beyond the basics, I suggest that you choose a study Bible for better detail and more exact wording of the original manuscripts. But for pure enjoyment of the Scriptures, a simpler version brings out the beautiful story of the Bible. There is nothing more fulfilling than sitting in a quiet place and reading the Scriptures alone with God. I hope these tools help you as much as they have helped me.

Chart 1:
DIVISION OF THE BOOKS OF THE BIBLE

OLD TESTAMENT BOOKS:
1. <u>History</u> (17)
   - a. Books of Law (5) — Genesis, Exodus, Leviticus, Numbers, and Deuteronomy
   - b. History (12) — Joshua, Judges, Ruth, 1 and 2 Samuel, 1 and 2 Kings, 1 and 2 Chronicles, Ezra, Nehemiah, and Esther
2. <u>Poetry</u> (5) — Job, Psalms, Proverbs, Ecclesiastes, and Song of Solomon
3. <u>Prophecy</u> (17)
   - a. Major Prophets (5) — Isaiah, Jeremiah, Lamentations, Ezekiel, and Daniel
   - b. Minor Prophets (12) — Hosea, Joel, Amos, Obadiah, Jonah, Micah, Nahum, Habakkuk, Zephaniah, Haggai, Zechariah, and Malachi

NEW TESTAMENT BOOKS:
4. <u>History</u> (5)
   - a. Gospels (4) — Matthew, Mark, Luke, and John
   - b. History (1) — Acts of the Apostles
5. <u>Letters</u> (21)
   - a. Paul's Letters (13) — Romans, 1 and 2 Corinthians, Galatians, Ephesians, Philippians, Colossians, 1 and 2 Thessalonians, 1 and 2 Timothy, Titus, and Philemon
   - b. General Letters (8) — Hebrews, James, 1 and 2 Peter, 1, 2 and 3 John, and Jude
6. <u>Prophecy</u> (1) — Revelation

See page 5 for explanation

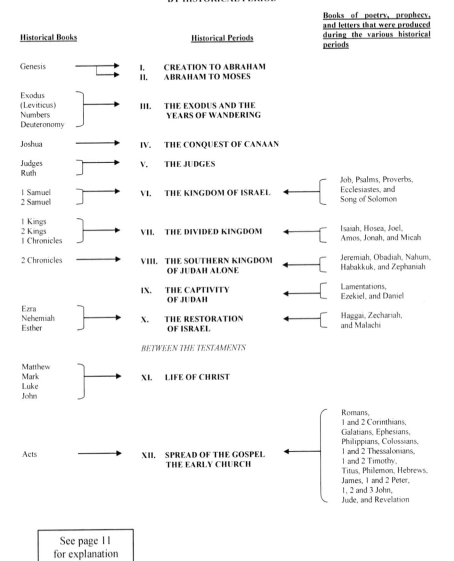

I. CREATION TO ABRAHAM   The Creation

                                           THE GARDEN
                                    Early Race of Mankind

II. ABRAHAM TO MOSES   Early Development of Israel
III. THE EXODUS AND THE   Moses Leadership
     YEARS OF WANDERING
IV. THE CONQUEST OF CANAAN   Joshua Leadership

V. THE JUDGES   12 Men and a Woman
                                    (Military Leaders)

VI. THE KINGDOM OF ISRAEL   King Saul (40)
                                           King David (40)
                                           King Solomon (40)

                                    Southern Kingdom of Judah

                                           Rehoboam (17)
                                           Abijah (3)
                                           Asa (41)

                                           Jehoshaphat
VII. THE DIVIDED KINGDOM   (25)

                                           Jehoram (8)
                                           Ahaziah (1)
                                           (Athaliah) (6)
                                           Joash (40)   Joel
                                                              Jonah
                                           Amaziah (29)   (Nineveh)
                                           Uzziah (52)

                                                         Isaiah
                                                         Micah
                                           Jotham (16)
                                           Ahaz (16)
                                           Hezekiah (29)

                                           Manasseh (55)
VIII. THE SOUTHERN KINGDOM   Amon (2)   Zephaniah
      OF JUDAH ALONE   Josiah (31)
                                           Jehoahaz (3m) Jeremiah
                                           Jehoiakim (11)   Nahum   (Nineveh)
                                           Jehoiachin (3m)   Obadiah (Edom)
                                           Zedekiah (11) Habakkuk

IX. THE CAPTIVITY   Babylonian Captivity (587 B.C.)
    OF JUDAH   Daniel
                           Ezekiel

X. THE RESTORATION   Return to Jerusalem from Captivity
   OF ISRAEL
                                           Zerubbabel   Haggai
                                           Ezra   Zechariah
                                           Nehemiah   Malachi

BETWEEN THE TESTAMENTS

XI. LIFE OF CHRIST
                                           THE CROSS

XII. THE ESTABLISHMENT OF
     THE EARLY CHURCH

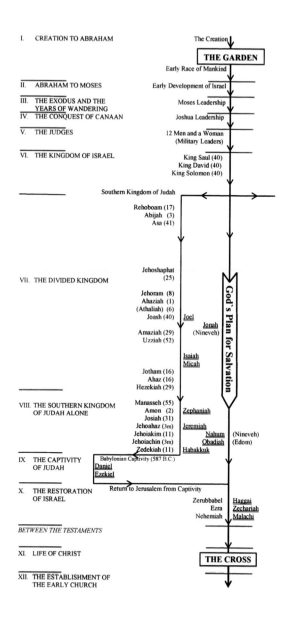

**Chart 3:
Bible Chronological
History Chart**

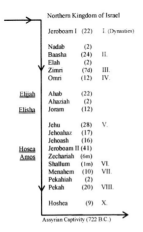

	Northern Kingdom of Israel		
	Jeroboam I	(22)	I. (Dynasties)
	Nadab	(2)	
	Baasha	(24)	II.
	Elah	(2)	
	Zimri	(7d)	III.
	Omri	(12)	IV.
Elijah	Ahab	(22)	
	Ahaziah	(2)	
Elisha	Joram	(12)	
	Jehu	(28)	V.
	Jehoahaz	(17)	
	Jehoash	(16)	
Hosea	Jeroboam II	(41)	
Amos	Zechariah	(6m)	
	Shallum	(1m)	VI.
	Menahem	(10)	VII.
	Pekahiah	(2)	
	Pekah	(20)	VIII.
	Hoshea	(9)	X.

Assyrian Captivity (722 B.C.)

See pages 12
for explanation

Short Overview of the Historical Books of the Bible

History Books of the Old Testament

- **Genesis**—The period from the beginning of creation to the reuniting of Jacob and Joseph in the land of Egypt
- **Exodus**—The four hundred years in Egypt in which Jacob's family grows into the Israelite nation, the going out of Egypt, The Ten Commandments, the tabernacle, and Shekinah glory
- **Leviticus**—All the Laws, sacrifices, and the ordinances of the priesthood
- **Numbers**—The Israelites wandering for forty years in the wilderness, Israel's journey to the Promised Land
- **Deuteronomy**—Moses's farewell addresses: recounting of history, God's solemn warnings to the Israelites
- **Joshua**—Conquest of Canaan led by Joshua, the division of the land among the twelve tribes of Israel
- **Judges**—First 300 years in the Promised Land: alternate oppressions and deliverances, God rules as a theocracy, "Everyone did as he saw fit"
- **Ruth**—God's protection of His people during the time of the Judges, the story of the great grandmother of David
- **The Samuels** (originally one book)
    - **1 Samuel**—The life of the final judge Samuel, the reign of Saul, David being crowned king and his flight from Saul
    - **2 Samuel**—The reign of David, conquering the land continues

- **The Kings** (originally one book)
  - **1 Kings**—The reign of Solomon, division of the Kingdom
  - **2 Kings**—The divided Kingdom, Elisha, captivity of the Northern Kingdom of Israel by Assyria, captivity of the Southern Kingdom of Judah by Babylon
- **The Chronicles** (originally one book)—Chronicles tells much of the same story as the books of Kings and Samuel, but Chronicles is not a history book. It retells the story of the Israelites from the time of David to captivity from a priestly perspective to show the exiles that they were still God's chosen people. To emphasize this point, Chronicles lists the genealogy back to Abraham to prove the lineage of God's chosen people. The northern kingdom Israel is not mentioned because they were not considered part of the chosen people.
  - **1 Chronicles**—Genealogies, the reign of David
  - **2 Chronicles**—Reign of Solomon, division of the Kingdom, emphasizing the history of Judah
- **Ezra:** Return from captivity, rebuilding of the Temple from Nebuchadnezzar's destruction of Jerusalem
- **Nehemiah:** Rebuilding of the wall of Jerusalem (Note: The book of Nehemiah is the final book of history in chronological order. After this, there is no more communication from God for some four hundred years until the announcement of the coming of John the Baptist.)
- **Esther:** A story from the time of the Mede–Persian captivity during the period of Restoration of Israel. It is a story of the Jews' deliverance from extermination.

History Books of the New Testament

- **The Gospels:** Stories of the life of Jesus from four different perspectives
    - **Matthew**: Jesus as the Messiah, written for Jews
    - **Mark:** Jesus as the Servant
    - **Luke:** Jesus as the Perfect Man
    - **John:** Jesus as Christ, the Son of God
- **Acts:** Establishment of the Early Church and spread of the Gospel to the Gentiles, life and work of Paul and other missionaries

Guide for Reading the History of the Bible

One of the best ways to grasp the *big picture* of the Bible is to read it! Here is a guide to reading through the history books to gain the big picture. Notice, this reading does not cover the entire Bible, but once you have grasped the story, the remainder of the books will be more easily understood. Each history book is put together in outline form to better help you connect the stories together. Some are more detailed than others, depending on the topic. So grab an easy read Bible like *The Living Bible* or the *Children's Bible: English Standard Version* and find a quiet place and enjoy reading. These types of Bibles, though not necessarily the best for in-depth study, are excellent for reading the Bible through to connect the stories. If you have never read just for the pure pleasure of reading the story, you are in for a treat. So grab your Bible and enjoy the most amazing story ever written.

I. **CREATION TO MOSES**
   - GENESIS (Read chs. 1–11): *Creation of the Earth, Beginning of Mankind, Fall of Man, The Flood, Tower of Babel*

II. **ABRAHAM TO MOSES**
   - GENESIS (Read chs. 12–50): *Beginning of the Hebrew Nation: Abraham, Isaac, Jacob, Joseph (The Patriarchs)*

III. **THE EXODUS AND THE YEARS OF WANDERING**
   - EXODUS (Read chs. 1–20): *Moses, Burning Bush, Ten Plagues, Crossing the Red Sea, Manna and Quail, Mount Sinai, Ten Commandments*
   - EXODUS (Skip chs. 21–31): *But know that Moses was called back up Mount Sinai (Ch. 24–31)*
   - EXODUS (Read ch. 32): *Events occurring at the base of Mount Sinai when Moses on top of the mountain*

- EXODUS (Read chs. 33–34): *Tent of Meeting, Second tablets, Renewed covenant*
- EXODUS (Read chs. 35–40): *Building of the Tabernacle*
- LEVITICUS (Skip): *Description of Feasts and Offerings*
- NUMBERS (Skip chs. 1–9) *The census and organization of the Israel camp*
- NUMBERS (Read chs. 10–14): *Murmurings, Twelve spies sent into the Promised Land, Ten spies bad report, Joshua and Caleb gave a report of faith, God's judgment*
- NUMBERS (Read chs. 15–20): *Moses's sin*, *The Forty Years in the Wilderness, Israel's Journey to the Promised Land*
- DEUTERONOMY (Skip chs. 1–32): *Moses Retelling the Story of the Exodus and Laws to the Israelites at the Entrance to the Promised Land, Solemn Warnings*
- DEUTERONOMY (Read chs. 33–34): *Moses Blesses the Tribes, Death of Moses, Joshua Succeeds*

IV. **THE CONQUEST OF CANAAN**
- JOSHUA (Read chs. 1–24): *The Conquest of Canaan, Rahab and the Spies, Crossing the Jordan, Fall of Jericho, Sun Made to Stand Still, Division of land among the Tribes*

V. **THE JUDGES**
- JUDGES (Read chs. 1–21): *Time of the Judges, A Cycle of Defeat, and Deliverance*
- RUTH (Read chs. 1–4): *The Kinsman Redeemer, Great-Grandmother of David*

VI. THE KINGDOM OF ISRAEL
- 1 SAMUEL (Read chs. 1–31): *Final Judge, Samuel, Reign of Saul*
- 2 SAMUEL (Read chs. 1–24): *The Reign of David*
- 1 KINGS (Read chs. 1–11): *The Reign of Solomon, The Temple, Solomon's Palace, Golden Age of Hebrew History*

VII. THE DIVIDED KINGDOM
- 1 KINGS (Read chs. 12–22): *The Kingdom Divides, Elijah*
- 2 KINGS (Read chs. 1–17): *The Lord Takes Elijah, Elisha, Captivity of the North Kingdom of Israel by Assyria*

VIII. JUDAH ALONE
- 2 KINGS (Read chs. 18–24:9): *Assyria Invades Judah, Isaiah, Deportations to Babylon, Jerusalem Destroyed*

IX. THE CAPTIVITY OF JUDAH
- 2 KINGS (Read chs. 24:10–25:30): *Captivity of Judah by Babylon*
- ESTHER (Read chs. 1–10): *The Jews' Deliverance from Extermination*

X. THE RESTORATION OF ISRAEL
- EZRA (Read chs. 1–10): *Return to The Promised Land, Temple Rebuilt, God's people repent*
- NEHEMIAH (Read chs. 1–13): *The Wall of Jerusalem Rebuilt*

XI. THE LIFE OF CHRIST
- MARK (Read chs. 1–16): *Jesus the Suffering Servant*

XII. THE ESTABLISHMENT OF THE EARLY CHURCH
- ACTS (Read chs. 1–28): *Formation and Spread of the Church, Persecution of Believers, Gospel goes to the Gentiles, Paul*

*My son, if you accept my words and store
up my commands within you,
Turning your ear to wisdom and applying
your heart to understanding,
And if you call out for insight and aloud for understanding,
And if you look for it as for silver and search
for it as for hidden treasure,
then you will understand the fear of the LORD
and find the knowledge of God*
(Proverbs 2:1–5).

CPSIA information can be obtained
at www.ICGtesting.com
Printed in the USA
FSOW01n1200220915
11407FS